Principles of
Christian Living

Answers to Some of
Life's Challenges

God Bless You!

Derek E. Eurales, Jr.

xulon
PRESS

1-11-2013

To Karen,

Thank you so much for all you do in the field of positive psychology. What your program taught me in the last several months has had a lasting impact on my life and relationships. May God continue to bless you with many more ideas and concepts to make the world around you better!

Your friend,

3 John 2

Contents

Endorsements

Staff Sergeant Derek Eurales Jr. is man of spiritual depth. And it comes out in his book as he winsomely speaks to the reader as if sitting together at a coffee table. But make no mistake, he will challenge you to be and receive all God desires for you.

Doug Ochner
Chaplain (CPT) US Army

Principles of Christian Living bring to remembrance strong opinions, views and facts in salvation, Christian living and faith. The author has composed a wellspring of knowledge to empower Gods chosen people "for the perfecting of the saints, for the work of the ministry, and the edifying of the body of Christ." Ephesians 4:12

Willie J. Curry
Pastor and Founder
Shekinah Tabernacle Ministries

First I want to give God the glory for allowing Elder Derek Eurales Jr. and his family to be a part of our lives. It is with great joy that I give thanks to our Father for this manuscript. As a Pastor I often look for materials to bless new believers in their walk. These 17 principles he lays out can be used as a tool for evangelism as well as new member's foundation. Elder Eurales has methodically laid the foundation for one seeking to know the Lord as his or her Savior and also for the growing child of the kingdom. These principles can even be put into track format for the lost. As I read his book, I could feel the transparency of his heart. As you read his book, you will know the Lord is assuring us we are not alone in our afflictions and there is an answer. 1 Peter 5:7-10

Bishop George F. Henfield
Pastor and Founder
Fellowship Temple Church of Hawaii

Derek Eurales Jr. has hit a home run for the Christian family. "Principles of Christian Living" is a "must" read for new believers and experienced Christians. This book provides a good foundation for new believers and motivation for those of us who may need an incentive to "press toward the mark for the prize of the high calling of God in Christ Jesus." (Philippians 3:14) This book has great significance for me because it was written by someone I know, love and respect. It contains eminent practical advice and will affirm, guide, and direct believers in every walk of life.

Dr. Dairy L. Williams
MISSION FOR TODAY

Other than the Bible, we've read many spiritual books and this book is the most inspiring. Our son is truly an anointed young writer. Our prayer is that he continues giving God the glory as he helps lead, encourage, and prepare you to do likewise. We love him and are so very proud of him!

Derek and Retha Eurales
Derek's Parents

Dedication

$\mathcal{T}$his book is dedicated to the memory of the men, women, boys and girls in my life who have gone on before me, and are now in the grandstands of time watching and waiting for that "Great Day" when we will all meet again.

Acknowledgements

*I*t is vitally important that we each have people in our lives who can minister to, encourage, correct, affirm and challenge us. With this in mind, I wish to thank some individuals who have impacted my life in a special way: First, my parents, Derek and Retha Eurales, who were my first mentors. Thank you to my grand-parents, Eugene Eurales, Shirley Davis, Judson and Minnie Childs, and Aunt Candy. You have all given me advice that I will value for eternity. Thanks also to Pastor Ronald Jones, the late Pastor Edward Jenkins, Bishop Paul Martin, Bishop George Henfield, Dr. Dairy Williams, Pastors George and Ollie Robinson, Pastor Marcus Davis, Pastor Willie Curry, Chaplain Doug Ochner and Mike Hill. Special thanks goes to my sisters, Patrona and Sheila, for not killing your little brother when you felt like it years ago and to my brother, DeVone, for always keeping it real. To my editor and the staff at Xulon, thanks for your help and expertise in the final stages of this book.

Now, to the greatest woman in the whole world, I offer the rest of my life in thanks. This is none other than my beautiful wife, Cecelia. I can't even put into words how much you mean to me. Thank you for praying for me. Your patience and belief in me makes me want to touch the clouds! To my girls, Kanesha, Carma, and Celeste, thanks for putting up with your dear old dad while I learn how to become the best dad I can. I love you all.

Introduction

*T*here are answers to our everyday challenges. Those answers are through first having a personal relationship with Jesus Christ, then by appropriating the help God already made available to us through Him.

Contained in this book are 17 lessons I learned in life as a believer that I want to pass on to you. The topics are tailored for situational victories as well as doctrinal application. My prayer is that you will find something encouraging and helpful in your walk with the Lord, and that you will also become a greater threat to the kingdom of darkness through applying these principles to your life.

In my writing, I make an attempt to communicate real issues that we face as humans as well as Christians. I use a number of "big words" throughout the book to get my point across. Please take it as an attempt on my part to use the best words possible to relay what God is saying. I believe "big words" have their place in literary works. So, if you encounter a word or two you don't understand, please enlist the help of a dictionary. It could only serve to enrich your life by increasing your vocabulary.

The Bible confirms in Philippians 4:13 *"I can do all things through Christ who strengthens me."* As you read each chapter, remember that you can be and do whatever God's Word says you can. Be blessed of God as you read further.

Derek E. Eurales, Jr.
February 29, 2004

Chapter #1

How to Receive Salvation

*W*hen I was a child, I was afraid of dying. I thought dying was extremely difficult to do. When I became of age, I found that death was the easy part of life. Life itself is one of the most perplexing experiences ever encountered by humans. Seeking the answers to life's problems alone can prove to be dangerous, even destructive (Proverbs 16:25). Consequently, finding those answers must begin in a personal relationship with God, through His Son Jesus Christ. This is what is meant by the term "being saved," and there are steps to receive this precious gift.

16 For God so loved the world that He gave His only begotten Son, that whoever believes in Him should not perish but have everlasting life. (John 3:16)

8 But what does it say? "The word is near you, in your mouth and in your heart" (that is, the word of faith which we preach): 9 that if you confess with your mouth the Lord Jesus and believe in your heart that God has raised Him from the dead, you will be saved. 10 For with the heart one believes unto righteousness, and with the mouth confession is made unto salvation. (Romans 10:8-10)

Before I explain the steps of salvation, I want to give you an understanding of what salvation is and why it is so important. Derived from the Hebrew word *"yeshu ah"* and the Greek word *"soteria,"* salvation is defined as "What God in mercy does for His sinful, finite human creatures." (International Dictionary of the Bible, Douglas & Tenney, p.887) [1]

In the beginning God created the heavens and the earth. (Gen. 1:1)

In verse eight of the same chapter, God called light into existence and made the firmament, which He called the heavens. God went on to define the different physical aspects of the Earth. He made the sun, the moon, and the stars also. The most significant thing God did in creation was making man in His own image, and then saying "...let them have dominion over the fish of the sea, and over the fowl of the air, and over the cattle, and over all the earth, and over every creeping thing..." (Vs. 26) God gave him a name, Adam, which means "of the earth" and also "the man." Adam was placed in charge of everything that was here on the Earth before him. In addition, Adam was given the right to name every living creature.

The Lord gave Adam specific instructions on what to eat and what not to eat. He also warned Adam in Gen. 2:17 that he would die the day that he ate of the tree of the knowledge of good and evil. The yielding to the temptation to eat of the tree occurs in Genesis chapter three. Until this point in scripture, man (humanity) had a perfect relationship with God. His disobedience to God caused sin to enter into the world.

Now, I know what you're thinking, gentlemen. "Didn't Eve play a part in all of this?" The answer is yes. However, the fault lies in the hands of "the man" because he was the one given the instructions. He had an opportunity to lead, but chose not to.

So when the woman saw that the tree was good for food, that it was pleasant to the eyes, and a tree desirable to make one wise, she took of its fruit and ate. She also gave to her husband with her, and he ate. (Genesis 3:6)

This scripture indicates that Adam was present during the whole conversation between the serpent and his wife. He could have stepped in and saved the day, but he did not. Instead, Adam kept silent, thus compromising his integrity and stepping out of his role. This left Eve with a decision, and she chose to step out of her rightful place and violate the command of God. It is when we as individuals step out of the place God has designed for us that we take on other roles not originally intended for us and run the risk of sinning also.

Your role is specific and distinct. You must be who the Lord purposed you to be. The cat can't be the dog any more than the moon can be the sun. God created everything with a purpose in mind. (Being outside of your purpose is not sin, but it is unfulfilling) All of creation has a message to preach in its own unique and individual way. That's the grandeur of God!

8 And they heard the sound of the Lord God walking in the garden in the cool of the day, and Adam and his wife hid themselves from the presence of the Lord God among the trees of the garden.9 Then the Lord God called to Adam and said to him, "Where are you?"10 So he said, "I heard Your voice in the garden, and I was afraid because I was naked; and I hid myself."11 And He said, "Who told you that you were naked? Have you eaten from the tree of which I commanded you that you should not eat?"(Genesis 3:8-11)

We each have to account for our own choices to operate either inside or outside of God's will. Because of God's mercy, He makes provisions for us even when we disobey Him. In Genesis 3:21, God made coats of animal skins and clothed Adam and Eve. This was the world's first shedding of blood for the remission of sins and covering of guilt. *(Job 29:14; Psalm 132:9; Matt. 26:28; Heb. 9:22)* God then ordered man to be put out of the Garden of Eden so that he could not eat of the tree of life and live forever in the same awful condition.

16And the Lord God commanded the man, saying, "Of every tree of the garden you may freely eat; 17 but of the tree of the knowledge of good and evil you shall not eat, for in the day that you eat of it you shall surely die." (Genesis 2:16-17)

Until they ate of the tree of knowledge of good and evil, there was free access in the Garden of Eden to the tree of life. Only when they decided to disobey God's restrictions was their amount of freedom in the garden and with God diminished considerably.

Since the fall of Adam, man has lived in a state of being unacceptable to God. Sin is a huge problem and if a person has a desire to be saved, he or she must first admit or acknowledge sin. If a person doesn't see that there is anything wrong with him or her, he or she will likely have a lifestyle that is characterized by an ability to present an incredible facade. A realization came over me one day – I was a sinner who needed the remedy, Jesus my Savior. Thank God someone shared the Word of God with me. Then, the Holy Spirit convicted my heart.

for all have sinned and fall short of the glory of God, (Romans 3:23)

Sin is what interferes with and nullifies a perfect relationship between God and humanity. In fact, the very consequence of sin without the remedy is death. (Romans 6:23) So, you first must realize that all have sinned and that your sins don't place you in a category by yourself. There are three ways a person sins; thoughts (Proverbs 24:9), words (Matthew 5:22), and actions (1 John 3:4). Again, the remedy for sin is Jesus Christ.

Next, you must repent. This means to be sorry. (To feel remorse or literally to make a U-turn back to God) It involves making a solemn vow to God to change your behavior. Please don't misunderstand. You can feel sorry for the wrong you've done without repentance. However, true repentance cannot come to be unless the sorrow is deeply rooted in sincere remorse for past misdeeds and a deep desire mixed with an active effort to change. This is a critical/life-changing step because God promises that people's sins will be blotted out when they repent. *(Acts 3:19)*

Along with repenting, you must confess with your own mouth that Jesus Christ is the Son of God and believe from the heart that He was made manifest in the flesh, overcame the temptations of this world, was crucified to make atonement for sin, and now sits on His throne in Heaven making all who believe in Him acceptable to God. (Rom. 8:34; Heb. 7:25; 1Tim 3:16)

Brace yourself! I will tell you now that you must give up committing acts that are not acceptable in God's plan for you. I know what you want to ask, "What's God's plan for me?" Well, my friend, God is revealing this to your spirit even as you read these pages. What you have to do is minimize the possibility of you not receiving God's best because of a part of your life that He's not pleased with. God has made an allowance for His people's lives to have a faultless and righteous foundation. Now, by this statement, I'm not saying that a person no longer has the power to sin once he gives his life to the Lord. The scripture above that states *"for all have sinned and fall short...,"* tells us that we all are susceptible to sinning. I am simply speaking to the foundation God set up for us.

[24] Now to Him who is able to keep you from stumbling, and to present you faultless before the presence of His glory with exceeding joy, [25] To God our Savior, who alone is wise, be glory and majesty, dominion and power, both now and forever. Amen. (Jude 24-25)

Because of God's love for us, he created us with the free will to choose our path. It is through the path of choosing Jesus that we can even begin to have a relationship with God. What we have to do is allow Jesus to present us faultless to the Father. Therefore, a renewal of the mind is necessary. (Rom 12:1-2)

There are sinful attributes that should not be part of the life of a believer in Christ. Lying and stealing are sins, and they should be replaced with truth and the will to labor for things desired. Corrupt communication is replaceable by words that edify others, and kindness can replace bitterness and wrath. These concepts are not always easy to fathom, much less live. Consequently, it would be beneficial to pray and ask God's help in removing all desire for sin.

[8] But what does it say? "The word is near you, in your mouth and in your heart" (that is, the word of faith which we

preach): ⁹ that if you confess with your mouth the Lord Jesus and believe in your heart that God has raised Him from the dead, you will be saved. ¹⁰ For with the heart one believes unto righteousness, and with the mouth confession is made unto salvation. (Romans 10:8-10)

These things I have written to you who believe in the name of the Son of God, that you may know that you have eternal life, and that you may continue to believe in the name of the Son of God. (1 John 5:13)

Finally, you've got to exhibit the faith and confidence in God to believe that you are saved. (1 John 5:13) The Bible, God's Holy Word, confirms that after confession and belief in Christ is established, a person is saved. (Rom. 10:9) There's not a more reliable printed source on the subject. Jesus said *"I am the way, the truth, and the life. No one comes to the Father except through Me." (John 14:6)* He also said, *"...for if you do not believe that I am He, you will die in your sins." (John 8:24)* Now, these were awesome claims to make. Only a crazy person would make these sorts of claims if they weren't true. So that leaves us with a dilemma. Who is Jesus? Is He who He said He is, or is He insane? I would submit to you the former rather than the latter.

Believing is the center of salvation. It will cause a supernatural transformation to take place in your life. Let me ask you this, if you die tonight, where will your soul spend the rest of eternity? Will it be Heaven - a place of peace, joy and rest in the eternal presence of God - or Hell - the place prepared for Satan and his angels that has enlarged itself for those who reject God's salvation? There's no place in between. Sadly, the hardest thing for many people to do is believe.

We are all faced with life changing decisions every day. Accepting salvation has proven to be the single most important choice of my life. God does not always give deliverance from all of life's troubles. However, He offers the best way to deal with them. (John 14:6)

This may all seem like a bit much to receive salvation. Trust me, it's really quite simple. Everything I just explained can be done in your heart, mind and mouth in about a minute. Right now, right here, wherever you are, is an opportunity for salvation. If you want to accept Jesus as your personal Savior, pray this prayer with me: *"Lord...I come to you now, a sinner. I'm sorry for the wrong I've done. According to Romans 10:9, I confess with my mouth the Lord Jesus and believe in my heart that you, God, have raised Him from the dead. And, based on my confession of faith, I believe now that I am saved, and that, according to 1 John 5:11, I have the promise of eternal life. I renounce the influence of Satan over my life. And I declare that I am a servant of God. Now, Lord, I pray that you will help me to grow into the person you are calling me to be. And I thank you. In Jesus' name I pray, Amen."*

Friend, if you've prayed this prayer today, you are saved! Let me be one of the first to welcome you into the family of God. Now, it's okay to not know everything about what just happened. None of us did when we accepted the Lord. In fact, I'm still trying to fully figure it all out. I still don't have all the answers. Just know that you now have eternal life according to 1 John 5:11. As soon as you can, find a strong Christian and tell him/her about what just happened. Then find a local church and request further guidance there. Also, utilize this book as encouragement. I hope you will receive a blessing by reading further. We all need people in our lives who can help us. Right now, it is crucial for you to make contact with those people. I'm convinced that this is the greatest decision you've ever made in your life! I'm very proud of you.

Endnote

[1] J.D. Douglas & Merrill C. Tenney, *The New International Dictionary of the Bible* (Grand Rapids, MI: The Zondervan Corporation, 1987), as listed under "Salvation," p. 887.

Chapter #2

Atonement

A wonderful thing happened to me one evening when I was at church. After feeling a deep desire to leave behind the sinful life I had been leading, I decided to accept Jesus Christ into my heart and began a relationship with God. The message of salvation was not a new one to me, being the son of a preacher. However, after I truly received salvation, the concept of Jesus "dying for my sins" took on a totally new meaning. I didn't know all of the details at first, but I knew that something was extremely different. Of course, the devil attacked me a number of times concerning past misdeeds, but God kept assuring me through his Word that *"There is therefore now no condemnation to those who are in Christ Jesus, who do not walk according to the flesh, but according to the Spirit." (Romans 8:1)*

The Lord wants us to know the significance of what was done for our sins. Because of Adam's disobedience to God, sin entered the world. Sin is what separates humanity from God. So man, in his separated state, is an enemy of God. Atonement is the act that brings together those who have been separated - enemies. One key word that applies to this fact is "propitiation." (Rom. 3:24-26) The root meaning of atonement in English is "reparation," which leads to the secondary meaning of reconciliation - "at-one-ment."

(Douglas & Tenney, p. 108) [1]

Under the Old Testament law of the atonement, the penalty due to the offender was transferred to an innocent animal to endure. The Hebrew word *"kopher"* means, "To cover" and is used generally in the sense of removing sin or defilement. This point parallels what the New Testament teaches about Christ, the Lamb of God. He was the innocent sacrifice who bore our sins – those of us who received His gift of salvation. Christ's fulfillment of this atonement is symbolized in the sixty-third chapter of Isaiah, verses one through nine. A more familiar passage is found in the third chapter of Zechariah where Christ - referred to as the "Angel of the Lord," the "righteous BRANCH," and the "stone with seven eyes" - revealed to Zechariah the cleansing of Joshua, the High priest.

The major difference between the Old Testament sacrifices and the New Testament sacrifice is the fact that the blood of animals could not take away sins. In fact, the taking away of sins could only come about through the shedding of the innocent blood of a perfect human life. The very best that the sacrifices of old could be used for was to temporarily cover the sin until a more perfect redemption came. (Doctrines, Pearlman, p. 192) [2] In Hebrews 10:1-18, it is explained how the old system of Jewish laws gave only a preview of the things Christ would do.

The sacrifices under the Old Testament system were repeated year after year but they didn't have the power to save those under their rules. What ended up happening was they were reminded on a yearly basis of their guilt and disobedience instead of relieving their minds. They needed a savior.

Christ understood that the sacrifice of animals and burnt offerings brought no special joy to God's heart. It was the life-devotion to service that God was, and still is, looking for. So in understanding this, Christ offered Himself as the once and for all sacrifice for sin. Under the New Testament system, there's no longer a need to offer more sacrifices to get rid of sins that have been forever forgiven and forgotten. (Heb. 10:18)

There are a number of things that the elements of Atonement are involved in and seen in. I will discuss four: Guilt transferred, Guilt removed, Forgiveness granted, and Righteousness given.

Guilt Transferred

Under the law as found in the Old Testament, there was a specific way that guilt was transferred. God gave the people instructions through Moses on what to do. They had to use animals from their flocks. The animal had to be a male and could not have any physical defects. The animal was to be brought to the entrance of the Tabernacle where the priest would accept the gift to the Lord. The person bringing the offering was to lay his hand upon the head of the animal, and by this the animal would become his substitute. Then, the person was to kill the animal. After the animal was killed, the priests were to bring the blood and sprinkle it around the altar at the entrance of the Tabernacle.

The sprinkling of the blood by the priest was symbolic of assuring the same promise of God to the forefathers, as outlined in Exodus chapter twelve and verse thirteen, and to those who the atonement was currently being made. *("And when I see the blood, I will pass over you.")* Next, the animal was to be skinned and put in sections, along with the fat and the head, upon a wood fire that was to be built upon the altar. The internal organs and legs of the animal were to be washed, and then burned upon the altar. The instructions for the transferal of guilt are seen in their entirety in the first chapter of Leviticus.

This process of atonement for sins was done all of the time and when it was first instituted it was a sweet smelling savor unto the Lord. However, after man's heart was examined, the sacrifices started "stinking." Under the New Testament system, Christ became the substitute, or ransom price, and the sins of the world were poured onto Him. (2 Corinthians 5:21)

Guilt Removed

[20] *"And when he has made an end of atoning for the Holy Place, the tabernacle of meeting, and the altar, he shall bring the live goat.* [21] *Aaron shall lay both his hands on the head of the live goat, confess over it all the iniquities of the children of Israel, and all their transgressions, concerning all their*

sins, putting them on the head of the goat, and shall send it away into the wilderness by the hand of a suitable man. [22] The goat shall bear on itself all their iniquities to an uninhabited land; and he shall release the goat in the wilderness. [23] "Then Aaron shall come into the tabernacle of meeting, shall take off the linen garments which he put on when he went into the Holy Place, and shall leave them there. [24] And he shall wash his body with water in a holy place, put on his garments, come out and offer his burnt offering and the burnt offering of the people, and make atonement for himself and for the people. [25] The fat of the sin offering he shall burn on the altar. [26] And he who released the goat as the scapegoat shall wash his clothes and bathe his body in water, and afterward he may come into the camp. (Leviticus 16:20-26)

As outlined in Leviticus chapter sixteen and verses twenty through twenty six, the guilt removal process dealt with the laying on of hands upon the head of a live goat by the priest, Aaron, and confessing over it all the sins of the people of Israel. The goat was then to be led by an appointed man into a land where no one lived and then released into the wilderness. So, when many people use the term "scapegoat" they are speaking of a scriptural principle and may not even know it.

Forgiveness Granted

[8] If we say that we have no sin, we deceive ourselves, and the truth is not in us. [9] If we confess our sins, He is faithful and just to forgive us our sins and to cleanse us from all unrighteousness. [10] If we say that we have not sinned, we make Him a liar, and His word is not in us. (1 John 1:8-9)

Forgiveness is granted as a free gift through Jesus and by confession. A person cannot earn salvation by works or by being good. God declares sinners to be good in His sight if they believe and have faith in Christ to save them. Psalm 32 talks about forgiveness and how blessed one is when his sins are covered. When people learn to stop hiding their sins and start admitting them to God, a great relief will overtake their lives. The Bible declares *"if we confess our sins, he is faithful and just to forgive us our sins, and to cleanse us from all unrighteousness." (1 John 1:9)*

Righteousness Given

Righteousness is given by God to the believer to bring him/her into a right standing with God. What happened in many churches was people were deceived by satanic influences into believing weekly church attendance and giving an offering was all they needed in order to qualify for Heaven. Is it because someone told them this is the way? In most cases, the answer is no. The primary reason for this way of thinking is because no one has taken the time to tell them, and show them, that this isn't the way. There is a hungry world waiting to be fed true spiritual food. The question is will we feed them?

Simply put, Atonement is making the guilty "not guilty" by divine sacrifice. It is important to know what was done for us by God through Christ Jesus. Knowing what one is a part of gives that person the extra motivation to "submit their bodies a living sacrifice, holy and acceptable unto God, which is his/her reasonable service."(Rom. 12:1

Endnotes

[1] J.D. Douglas & Merrill C. Tenney, *The New International Dictionary of the Bible* (Grand Rapids, MI: The Zondervan Corporation, 1987), as listed under "Atonement," p. 108.

[2] Myer Pearlman, *Knowing the Doctrines of the Bible* (Springfield, MO: Gospel Publishing House, 1937, 1981), as listed under "The Atonement," p. 192.

Chapter #3

God's Provisions for Living

*A*s outlined in the scriptures, spiritual gifts come from God, (Jas. 1:17), and are assigned sovereignty by His choosing. (1Cor. 12:11, 28) In understanding these things, one must also understand that spiritual gifts cannot be bought or earned; only received. They are always for the edification of others, (Rom. 1:11; 1 Pet. 4:10), and are spiritually discerned. (1Cor 12:2, 3)

God is, without a doubt, "The Giver." In addition to the every day material things made possible - food, water, health, rest, shelter - God has given us several very special spiritual provisions. Seven of these special gifts to humanity will be discussed here.

The Best Gift

The single most important gift that God has given is Christ, His son. It is through Christ that man has a chance to get to know God in a personal way. The Bible states in John 3:16 *"For God so loved the world that He gave His only begotten Son, that whoever believes in Him should not perish but have everlasting life."*

Power for Witnessing

As Christians, we have been given a commission. (Matthew

28:19-20) By accepting Christ, there is an assurance of eternal life in Heaven, but God wants more people to receive this assurance and it is by way of our witness. Since we are but humans, God has given the Holy Spirit (Luke 11:13) who provides power for witnessing. (Acts 1:8)

Grace

God has also given His divine unmerited favor, which is called grace. (James 4:6) This grace is descriptive of God's forgiving mercy (Romans 11:6) and is the source of salvation (Acts 15:11), of faith (Acts 18:27; Ephesians 2:8), and of justification. (Romans 3:24) The Apostle Paul described Grace as being undeserved. (1Timothy 1:12-16)

Wisdom

Wisdom is given to those who simply ask for it. James 1:5 says *"If any of you lacks wisdom, let him ask of God, who gives to all liberally and without reproach, and it will be given to him."* Still and all, there are instructions in receiving wisdom that must be followed carefully. Continue reading verses 6 - 8 of the same chapter. Also, reference Proverbs 4:5-7.

Eternal Life

God has established a way for the whole world to receive eternal life (John 10:28), and that way is through the God-given gift of repentance and faith. It is wonderful to know that everyone has the opportunity to repent of past wrongdoings, believe in Jesus Christ and come into a right relationship with God, thus receiving eternal life. (Acts 11:18; Romans 10:9-10)

God's Peace

God's peace has been given to those who have received Christ into their lives. (Isaiah 53:5) Psalm 29:11 says *"The Lord will give*

strength to His people; the Lord will bless His people with peace."
Those who have not come to know Christ personally do not have
the privilege of experiencing true peace. (Isaiah 48:22) Once the
child of God receives from God the peace that surpasses all understanding (Philippians 4:7), he is able to have peace in all circum-
stances of life. The entire fourth chapter of Philippians should be
studied in order to get a clearer understanding of these truths.

God's Place of Rest

The fourth chapter of Hebrews talks about the requirements of
entering God's rest and how acceptance of this rest must be
combined with faith. (Verse 2) We can miss out on God's rest if we
are full of unbelief and disobedience to His Word. (Verses 3-11)
Jesus tells us to come to Him and receive rest through His instruction. (Matt. 12:28-30)

God is faithful. He continues to give us what we need on a
continual basis and all He wants in return is for us to make the
choice to serve Him. That's LOVE.

Chapter #4

The Intentions of Satan

Satan is powerful, but he's not all-powerful. (Not omnipotent) Satan is smart. I'll go so far as to say he's even smarter than you and I at times, but he doesn't know everything. (Not omniscient) Satan can be in a lot of places, but he is not everywhere at all times. (Not omnipresent) Only God possesses these eternal and sovereign attributes, and, because of the fact that Satan does not, he will always attempt to thwart the plans that God has for the lives of the believers. It's in his rebellious nature to do so. In view of this knowledge, today, a number of tactics Satan uses and what he intends to do will be exposed so that the committed children of God will be thoroughly equipped to do good things! (2 Timothy 3:17)

The Counterfeit

14 And no wonder! For Satan himself transforms himself into an angel of light. (2 Corinthians 11:14)

Since Satan lacks the necessary qualities found in God, he has to disguise himself. For every "Live," there is a "Memorex." For every "real" there is a "counterfeit." By disguising himself and his demons, Satan can present a righteous appearance and deceive many into taking his crooked advice.

Satan wants to undo God's work. This is mainly because of the pride that led to his rebellion and subsequent ousting from heaven. (Ezekiel 28:15; Isaiah 14:13-14) The scriptures are given by God's inspiration. They instruct God's people in righteousness. (2 Timothy 3:16-17) A person who studies the Word and prays continually is a strong and mature Christian. Satan's intentions are to distract the child of God from following the every day disciplines of reading and studying the Word of God and praying. He would also love for you and I to forget God's promises that come by way of the Word so that we can't make it to the place of maturity God has already ordained. This is why we have to allow the Word to take root within us! (Matthew 13:3-9)

May he make a Suggestion?

Suggestive tactics often accomplish the intentions of Satan. A lot of us find ourselves to be most tired when reading the Bible and end up falling asleep when God is trying to talk to us. Many times we find ourselves to be most busy when there is kingdom work to be done. (Things done for God's glory) The parable of the soils in the fourth chapter of Mark illustrates this point. (Namely, verse 15)

The Instigator of Evil

Another intention of Satan is to instigate evil. This is seen in his suggestion to Judas Iscariot to carry out his plan to betray Jesus. (John 13:2, 27) Satan uses the same tactics today. Although sin is a choice, many choose to take suggestions from the devil and cause confusion and commotion.

One might ask, "How does one know if he or she is taking suggestions from the devil?" As stated before, Satan is a counterfeit. He is very cunning and can use his persuasiveness to fool people into believing half-truths – lies mixed with enough of the truth to make sin justifiable in their own eyes. (Matthew 4:6) So, it is very important to measure everything said and done by the Word of God. (1 John 4:1-6)

The Bottom Line

Satan's ultimate goal is to secure men's worship for himself. He tried to exalt himself above God and got kicked out of Heaven. (2 Thessalonians 2:3-12; Luke 10:18; Isaiah 14) He tried to get Jesus to worship him and was unsuccessful. (Luke 4:6-8) Satan would deceive the most mature Christian if it were possible. (Matthew 24:24) However, the serious believer – a person who fervently pursues his or her relationship with God – is not ignorant of his devices (2 Corinthians 2:11), so Satan remains a defeated foe. Two questions: are you a serious believer? And, do you possess the determination to get the most out of your relationship with the Lord? If the answers to these questions are yes, you can defeat your enemy, the devil. God will show you how.

Chapter #5

Elements of Worship

*W*orship is an act of respect, reverence, or adoration. In the Hebrew, it is 'shahah' - bow down, prostrate. In the Greek, it is 'proskyneo' - to prostrate, do obeisance to. The English word means 'worth-ship' and denotes the worthiness of the individual receiving the special honor. (Douglas & Tenney, p. 1070) [1] Douglas & Tenney also define worship as "the honor, reverence, and homage paid to superior beings or powers, whether men, angels, or God." That's why it is extremely important to understand worship in the life of a Christian and how and to whom it should be given.

> [20] *Our fathers worshiped on this mountain, and you Jews say that in Jerusalem is the place where one ought to worship."* [21] *Jesus said to her, "Woman, believe Me, the hour is coming when you will neither on this mountain, nor in Jerusalem, worship the Father.* [22] *You worship what you do not know; we know what we worship, for salvation is of the Jews.* [23] *But the hour is coming, and now is, when the true worshipers will worship the Father in spirit and truth; for the Father is seeking such to worship Him.* [24] *God is Spirit, and those who worship Him must worship in spirit and truth." (John 4:20-24)*

He is Worthy

To worship God is to recognize His worth or worthiness and to acknowledge His value. The time will come when people will be more concerned with how to worship than where to worship. The Father wants His people's worship to be spiritual and real. This must be accomplished through the assistance of the Holy Spirit. (John 4:23-24)

It is the job of the Christian to be an active worshiper of God. True worship requires the involvement of five basic elements. The first element is praising God for all that He is and all He has done. God's acts on this earth are unequaled. Psalm 150:2 says *"Praise Him for His mighty acts; praise Him according to His excellent greatness!"*

Acknowledging His Goodness

Along with praise comes thanksgiving for His gifts and goodness. The entire ninety-fifth number of Psalm is a call to worship the Lord who controls everything. Verse two says *"Let us come before his presence with thanksgiving; let us shout joyfully to Him with psalms."* The Bible declares also in Philippians 4:6 *"Be anxious for nothing, but in every thing by prayer and supplication, with thanksgiving, let your requests be made known to God."* God is good, and when you acknowledge His goodness it brings Him even closer to your situation and prepares the atmosphere for an exchange to take place. The result of the exchange is the answering and fulfillment of your requests.

The Offering

The third element involved with worshipping is offering of one's gifts, services, and whole self to the Lord. It is the duty of true Christians to yield their vessels - bodies - to the use of God. (Romans 12:1) God uses the ordinary things of this world to bring glory to Himself and at the same time causes His people to grow into a deeper relationship with Him. (1 Corinthians 1:18-31)

Obeying His Voice

Fourth, one must learn from the Word of God and obey His voice. In Exodus 19:5, God says this to the people of Israel: *"Now therefore, if you will indeed obey My voice and keep My covenant, then you shall be a special treasure to Me above all people; for all the earth is Mine."* All that is learned and experienced in the physical process of worshipping the Almighty God should line up with the Word. (1 John 4:1-6) By the same principle, all that is learned and experienced in the Word of God should lead us into worship. (Psalm 95:6)

Proclaiming God's Worth

I explained earlier that worship is derived from the English term "worth-ship." True worship cannot be complete without telling others about God's worth. Many of us live our lives as if God's grace is only big enough to cover our own sins and no one else's. When the child of God fails to witness, tell of God's goodness, he is quenching - or smothering - the spirit of God and thus preventing the completeness of a total worship experience in his life. (1 Thessalonians 5:19) This truth alone is what prevents many from moving to the proverbial place called "higher in the Lord."

There are a number of patterns of worship found in Christian assemblies around the world. Most of them are right and good. The real test, however, is whether one's involvement in worship is pure. As the 'serious believer' strives to remain serious in his devotion to God, there is a need to not only get wisdom. He must also *"get understanding."* (Proverbs 4:7)

Praise Is How We Get Our Raise

Psalm 33:1 Rejoice in the Lord, O ye righteous: for praise is comely for the upright.

Child of God, there are so many things in our lives that we are concerned about, but God's Word tells us to "Rejoice." Don't you know that it's best to praise the Lord even when you don't feel good? James 1:2-3 says *"...count it all joy when you fall into various trials, ³ knowing that the testing of your faith produces patience"* Our enemy, the devil, doesn't want us to praise God in times of difficulty because even he knows that there is power, deliverance, victory and joy in praise.

The Key

Here's the key: when the trials, temptations and obstacles come...operate in a "Blessed Assurance" that everything is going to be all right. Whatever the problem, whatever the situation, just know that when you praise the Lord simply for who He is and all He is to you, your deliverance from the worry of life's troubles is just around the corner. Notice, I didn't say deliverance from life's troubles. I said deliverance from the worry. (Philippians 4:7)

One Verse Bandits

Psalm 34:1 I will bless the Lord at all times: his praise shall continually be in my mouth.

Many Christians quote this scripture quite often. The problem is many of us are guilty of being "O.V.Bs." Short for "One Verse Bandits," this is a condition where an individual will only read one verse in a particular book of the Bible without ever taking the time to find any deeper revelation in the rest of the book.

I'll be one of the first to admit I was guilty in the past, but I try my absolute best to not let the O.V.B. mentality overshadow my life as a believer. That's why I am now able to define it and talk about it. When you stick to one verse that you like, sooner or later it becomes a major part of your life as a believer. That's not wrong if your spiritual diet involves a balance of the whole of the scriptures. If this is not the case, you will only limit your growth. Just remember, *"All Scripture is given by inspiration of God, and is profitable for doctrine, for reproof, for correction, for instruction in righteousness." (2 Timothy 3:16)*

Now, granted, the message of salvation and hope for the world is wrapped up into one verse, John 3:16. So, I'm not saying that you should throw away your practice of feasting on one particular scripture in your devotional time with God. I'm simply stating that there are many areas in the Bible where God wants you to understand the full context of what is being said in order to relate and communicate life-changing principles of living. Many times, this can only be done through an understanding of a whole passage versus one verse.

Endnote

[1] J.D. Douglas & Merrill C. Tenney, *The New International Dictionary of the Bible* (Grand Rapids, MI: The Zondervan Corporation, 1987), as listed under "Worship," p. 1070.

Chapter 6

Personal Requirements of Prayer

*P*rayer is communicating with God. There are five basic parts of prayer. (Not ranked by order) The first part is adoration, which is to love intensely. In adoring God, the person is acknowledging God for who He is. A good example of this is found in Daniel 4:34-35. Second, confession must take place. (1 John 1:9) Next is supplication - making of humble requests. (Philippians 4:6; Ephesians 6:18; Psalm 6:9) Then, there's intercession - prayer offered in behalf of others. (James 5:14, 15; Ex. 32:11-13) Finally, there's thanksgiving. (Phil. 4:6; Eph. 5:20)

Be not deceived. Before the elements of a prayer life can work, an understanding of and compliance with the personal requirements involved must be established. Jesus gives the following example of how to pray in Matthew 6:5-15:

5 "And when you pray, you shall not be like the hypocrites. For they love to pray standing in the synagogues and on the corners of the streets, that they may be seen by men. Assuredly, I say to you, they have their reward. 6 But you, when you pray, go into your room, and when you have shut your door, pray to your Father who is in the secret place; and your Father who sees in secret will reward you openly. [7] And when you pray, do not use vain repetitions as the heathen do. For they think that they will be heard for their many words. [8] "Therefore do not be like them. For your Father knows the things you have need of before you ask Him. [9] In this manner, therefore, pray: Our Father in heaven, Hallowed be Your name. [10] Your kingdom come. Your will be done On earth as it is in heaven. [11] Give us this day our daily bread. [12] And forgive us our debts, As we forgive our debtors. [13] And do not lead us into temptation, But deliver us from the evil one. For Yours is the kingdom and the power and the glory forever. Amen. [14] "For if you forgive men their trespasses, your heavenly Father will also forgive you. [15] But if you do not forgive men their trespasses, neither will your Father forgive your trespasses.

Purity of Heart

[18] If I regard iniquity in my heart, The Lord will not hear. [19] But certainly God has heard me; He has attended to the voice of my prayer. [20] Blessed be God, Who has not turned away my prayer, nor His mercy from me! (Psalm 66:18-20)

God is not inclined to listen to the prayer of a person who has un-confessed sins. It is only those who have a right relationship with God, through repentance and confession of Jesus Christ, who will be heard by God. Honesty before God is vital.

I can't speak for everyone. I just know that it's wonderful knowing God hears my prayers.

Believing

There is great power in believing! In the Bible, many miraculous things were done because of belief. The people of God were given a conditional promise of being established and prosperous if they would believe in the Lord and in His prophets. (2 Chronicles 20:20) Jairus' daughter was healed after Jesus told him "Be not afraid, only believe." (Mark 5:36) Jesus restored sight to two blind men when they confirmed that they believed He could do it. (Matthew 9:28-29) Christ guarantees that when people pray with a pure heart and believe that they will receive what they are praying for, it will be done. (Mark 11: 20-24)

A Forgiving Spirit

There is a need for all Christians to know how to forgive. A person of prayer must be an active exerciser of forgiveness. Romans 3:23 says, *"for all have sinned and fall short of the glory of God."* In this particular scripture, the word "fall" is indicative of the present condition of man without Jesus. No human is above error. At some point or another in life, there will be a need for forgiveness. It is important to note that God will not forgive the sins of a person who does not exercise forgiveness toward others in his or her daily prayer life. (Matthew 6:14; Mark 11:25-26; Psalm 32:1-2; 2 Corinthians 2:10)

In His Name

There is all power and authority in the name of Jesus. Deeds that are done in Christ's name are rewarded. (Matthew 10:42) Christ's name alone brings glory to the Father because of what He did in coming to the world and making the once-and-for all atonement for the sins of humanity. (John 14:13-14) Therefore, man's present condition with Christ is not "fallen," but "lifted up." The authority of Christ's name will bring God's attention to prayers.

According to God's Will

Observe this scenario: Jimmy is a twenty-two year old man with a job as a cashier at a local department store. He makes roughly $1,500 per month. He is a born again believer in Jesus Christ. He has a desire to purchase a brand new luxury car valued at $46,000.

Even though he's a believer and has asked God for the car "in the Name of Jesus," God's will for the young man at this point in his life would more likely be a nice economy car priced somewhere between $12,000 and $15,000.

As people of God continually study the Word and search out God's will for their lives, the wisdom to pray according to His will comes. (1 John 3:22; 5:14-15; Ephesians 5:17) Fulfilling personal requirements in prayer allows for a mighty move of God on the behalf of all involved whether in secret, as a family, in a small group, or in public.

Chapter 7

"Intending To Pray In A Focused, Targeted, And Faith-Filled Way"

To intend means to be purposed, resolved, and determined. To focus means to bring together to a principle centre. A target is a mark to aim at in shooting. To be faith-filled means to believe one's prayers are answered according to that person's relationship with God. This is said in James 5:15-16 from the Life Application Bible: *"And their prayer, if offered in faith, will heal him, for the Lord will make him well; and if his sickness was caused by some sin, the Lord will forgive him. Admit your faults to one another and pray for each other so that you may be healed. The earnest prayer of a righteous man has great power and wonderful results."*

So, to say that we intend to pray in a focused, targeted, and faith-filled way means this: (1.) that we are purposed and determined to bring together the anointing that God has placed on all of our lives, (2.) that we are to be specific with our requests to God, and (3.) that we are to base the answer of those prayers on our own personal relationship with God through His Word.

37Nay, in all these things we are more than conquerors through him that loved us. (Romans 8:37)

In our prayer life, it is important to realize that we have nothing to be afraid of. We must pay attention to the things that concern our brothers and sisters so that we can know how to target our prayers. There are two elements needed in successful corporate intercession:

Obedient Spirit

19 If you are willing and obedient, you shall eat the good of the land; 20 but if you refuse and rebel, you shall be devoured by the sword; for the mouth of the Lord has spoken. (Isaiah 1:19-20)
17 But God be thanked that though you were slaves of sin, yet you obeyed from the heart that form of doctrine to which you were delivered. 18 And having been set free from sin, you became slaves of righteousness. (Romans 6:17-18)

In the Christian life, true obedience comes from the heart. It opens the door for us to learn more of God. He really does desire for us to get to know Him better. (John 14:21)

Unity

3 endeavoring to keep the unity of the Spirit in the bond of peace. 4 There is one body and one Spirit, just as you were called in one hope of your calling; 5 one Lord, one faith, one baptism; 6 one God and Father of all, who is above all, and through all, and in you all. (Ephesians 4:3-6)

25 But Jesus knew their thoughts, and said to them: "Every kingdom divided against itself is brought to desolation, and every city or house divided against itself will not stand. (Matthew 12:25)

One thing that breaks my heart about Christendom is that the body, as a whole, is not unified. Too many times, we allow conflict caused by minor disagreements to separate us. This is the "divide and conquer" principle the devil employs against the body. We must allow the Holy Spirit to lead and unite us so that our prayers can be effective. It is vitally important to depend on our personal relationship with God through His Word and not with people when receiving the answers to our prayers.

We must all make a concerted effort to be one, even as Christ and the Father are one. (John 17:11) We have to pray for unity in the body and then do the things that bring it about. We must challenge negative statements made to us or around us about the church, the ministry, fellow believers and so on. If every Christian began praying for unity in the body, it would definitely close the gap on the division we face today. The thing is, we are already one. (Ephesians 4:3-6) We just have to realize it and keep the unity. I offer this prayer: *"Father... I come to you now in thanksgiving for all that you've done in my life and in the life of my friend who's reading along. You are so wonderful, kind and patient with me. I acknowledge your commandment that we, according to John 13:34, are to love one another even as you have loved us. I confess that I don't have all the answers, but in your strength I can do all things. Help us all to be more like Jesus, to do the things that bring about unity in the body. I thank you again. In Jesus' name, Amen."*

Chapter 8

Pulling Down Strongholds

"How to Follow Peace"

Therefore we also, since we are surrounded by so great a cloud of witnesses, let us lay aside every weight, and the sin which so easily ensnares us, and let us run with endurance the race that is set before us, (Hebrews 12:1)

Strong holds- things that prevent Christians from finding true happiness in God. (Sin)

Humans use human plans and methods to solve their problems. However, these means don't always ensure positive results. God wants us all to use His mighty weapons to thwart the evil plans of the devil. One of these weapons is peace. God's peace will always counter the devil's intentions of stirring up strife amongst brethren. The most important truth about peace in the life of a believer in Christ is the fact that we must not simply know about it. We must also possess it.

14 Pursue peace with all people, and holiness, without which no one will see the Lord: (Hebrews 12:14)

It is true that one who is not holy won't see the Lord. It is also easy to quote scriptures such as Hebrews 12:14 when it applies to life. Still, one needs to know how to apply the spiritual truths found inside of the Word of God to really experience the victory over the enemy. If not, one is simply quoting the scriptures with no power.

Peace is the absence of war or other hostilities; an agreement or treaty to end hostilities; freedom from quarrels and disagreement; harmonious relations. The following is not meant to be an exhaustive volume of information, but a little encouragement to help you in the pursuit of following peace. Here are two keys:

1. Renew your commitment to God on a consistent basis (have peace with God). Romans 5:1; 1 Corinthians 15:31; Romans 12:1-2; Colossians 3:15

2. Remain Calm (have the peace of God) Matthew 5:25; Proverbs 15:1; Philippians 4:7

It takes a lot of patience to be peaceable with some people. When a Christian flies off the handle, it shows that he or she has stepped out of control. Christians demonstrate a level of God's control in their lives when they can remain calm in the midst of conflict. What will you do?

Chapter 9

How to Live When Others Are Expecting You to Die

8 We are hard-pressed on every side, yet not crushed; we are perplexed, but not in despair; 9 persecuted, but not forsaken; struck down, but not destroyed— 10 always carrying about in the body the dying of the Lord Jesus, that the life of Jesus also may be manifested in our body. 11 For we who live are always delivered to death for Jesus' sake, that the life of Jesus also may be manifested in our mortal flesh. 12 So then death is working in us, but life in you. 13 And since we have the same spirit of faith, according to what is written, "I believed and therefore I spoke," we also believe and therefore speak, 14 knowing that He who raised up the Lord Jesus will also raise us up with Jesus, and will present us with you. (2 Corinthians 4:8-15)

The Extra Effort

You need to realize that your life is worth the struggle (extra effort). A famed song says, "We're living this life just to live

53

again." This is true. Our life matters because there are people (lost souls) we encounter every day who hunger and thirst for a spiritual awakening and don't even know it. One way you can tell is when you are in the presence of some people and the conversation changes. Their speech becomes nicer. They may or may not know you're saved, but they know something is different about you. (Their conscience tells them) They respect the anointing of God on your life enough to want to come up to your level.

The conscience of unsaved people is appealed to by none other than the Holy Ghost operating through God's initial call to come to the Lord. (John 16:8-10) Even if you don't have these kinds of encounters, or you're reading this today and you're not saved, don't feel bad. Your life matters to God and you will have the opportunity to receive Christ into your life in just a few moments. (Refer to Chapter 1) If you're already saved, you now have an opportunity to make a positive step toward a closer walk with God. That's what this book is all about: receiving answers to help one obtain the freedom in life God intended. Hopefully you'll see that as you read.

Turn your face to the wall

In those days Hezekiah was sick and near death. And Isaiah the prophet, the son of Amoz, went to him and said to him, "Thus says the Lord: 'Set your house in order, for you shall die, and not live.' " 2 Then he turned his face toward the wall, and prayed to the Lord, saying, 3 "Remember now, O Lord, I pray, how I have walked before You in truth and with a loyal heart, and have done what was good in Your sight." And Hezekiah wept bitterly. 4 And it happened, before Isaiah had gone out into the middle court, that the word of the Lord came to him, saying, 5 "Return and tell Hezekiah the leader of My people, 'Thus says the Lord, the God of David your father: "I have heard your prayer, I have seen your tears; surely I will heal you. On the third day you shall go up to the house of the Lord. 6 And I will add to your days fifteen years. I will deliver you and this city from the hand of the king of Assyria; and I will defend this city for My own sake, and for the sake of My servant David. (2 Kings 20:1-6)

Hezekiah was 25 years old when he began to reign in Judah, a nation plagued by its own decisions to follow the ways of a corrupt society. His 29-year reign was characterized by doing right in the sight of the Lord. He did a house cleaning.

5 He trusted in the Lord God of Israel, so that after him was none like him among all the kings of Judah, nor who were before him. (2 Kings 18:5)

Notice in 2 Kings 20:2 that Hezekiah didn't take the time to argue with Isaiah. He went directly to the wall. There are some things involved with turning your face to the wall. (a) First, you're not focusing on what people say (The "they say" syndrome). We sometimes worry too much about "they say." Who is "they say" anyway? Let's be real. If you have a terminal illness, people are expecting you to die. But you don't have to die. God is ABLE to heal you. The Bible tells us prophetically in Isaiah 53:4-5 that Christ has already borne our sickness and pain. Jesus Himself took on the punishment we deserved because of our inherent connection to Adam and Eve and because He took our punishment, we can live. (b) Secondly, you're not concerned about tripping over anything because you've got your face to the wall. Your posture when dealing with problems will determine the impact they have on you. (c) Thirdly, you're looking away from your problems and looking unto Jesus... the author and finisher of our faith. (Heb. 12:1-2)

Pray

6 Be anxious for nothing, but in everything by prayer and supplication, with thanksgiving, let your requests be made known to God; (Philippians 4:6)

16 Confess your trespasses to one another, and pray for one another, that you may be healed. The effective, fervent prayer of a righteous man avails much. (James 5:16)

We often leave prayer out in our initial stages of dealing with our problems. One reason is because many of us have a selfish desire to remain in control and solve our own problems. Despite our attempts to remain self-sufficient in every aspect of our lives, prayer is vitally important because it connects us with Almighty God. The sincere prayers of a person with a right relationship with God mean a lot to God. We find in 2 Kings 20:6 that God added 15 more years to Hezekiah's life.

Be willing to Persevere

Let's look at Mark 5:25-34. There was a woman with an issue of blood for 12 years. Jesus was on His way to heal Jairus' 12-year-old daughter. But, on the way he encountered a crowd of people and this woman who had been bleeding as long as the little girl had been living. This lady had problems. No money-No man. But in spite of what she didn't have, she pressed and got her blessing.

In 1 Corinthians 4:8-15, the apostle Paul talked about the trials they faced in ministry and the rewards and benefits they had and were looking forward to. So, how do we live when others are expecting us to die? We just have to make a decision to trust God.

While you're reading this, you may or may not be facing a trial that you don't have the answer to. Pray this prayer: *"Lord...I come to you asking that you help me to face the wall when I don't understand, and give me the assurance that everything will be alright. In Jesus' name, Amen."* God is standing by waiting for you to give whatever problems you have to Him. He won't leave you or fail you. If you're not saved, read Romans 10:9 and accept Jesus today. Do it now! (See the prayer at the end of chapter one)

Chapter 10

He Placed His Hand On Me

"A Personal Agent, Taking Personal Action"

⁵ You have hedged me behind and before, and laid your hand upon me. (Psalm 139:5)

⁸ and a letter to Asaph the keeper of the king's forest, that he must give me timber to make beams for the gates of the citadel which pertains to the temple, for the city wall, and for the house that I will occupy." And the king granted them to me according to the good hand of my God upon me. ¹⁸ And I told them of the hand of my God which had been good upon me, and also of the king's words that he had spoken to me. So they said, "Let us rise up and build." Then they set their hands to this good work. (Nehemiah 2:8, 18)

¹⁹ "All this," said David, "the Lord made me understand in writing, by His hand upon me, all the works of these plans." (1 Chronicles 28:19)

²⁹ My Father, who has given them to Me, is greater than all; and no one is able to snatch them out of My Father's hand. (John 10:29)

Also, reference Acts 4:23-31.

Agency- Business that acts for others

Agent- One who acts as the representative for another

It's amazing what can be done under a mighty touch from God. In the instance of Acts chapter four, the Apostles needed boldness to proclaim the Word of God at a time when they were being commanded not to. Their lives were in danger because of this Gospel they were preaching. They asked God for what they needed and they got it. They received another empowerment to turn the world upside down.

We've got to understand the personal agency of God. How does one stay positive in a world that is so negative? How does one stay encouraged in a world that is so disheartening? How do you encourage? How do you strengthen? How do you build? How do you smile? How do you make things better? How do you make it real?

In our lives there are instances where we feel we are not getting the simple satisfaction of a fair shake. It's at those times that we sometimes feel the need to take matters into our own hands. But we've got to understand that we have security in the capable hands of God. He is a personal agent who is taking personal action. You see, when God stretches out His hand, it means that He is getting involved in whatever the situation may be. Don't worry! Don't fret! You are special to God! 1 Samuel 12:22 affirms " *22 For the Lord will not forsake His people, for His great name's sake, because it has pleased the Lord to make you His people."*

No one is able to undo what God has done. No one is able to tear down what God has established. Are you saved? Are you born again? If so, guess what? God has set you up. He has established you in the body of Christ, and nobody can undo it. No weapon formed against you will prosper. God <u>has</u> placed His hand on YOU!

When there are things that start to affect us, and we call upon the Lord for help, God takes those things personal and begins to take action. I am a man of God. I am strong. I am prosperous. I am successful. I am an over achiever, I am more than a conqueror because He is my personal agent, taking personal action, He placed His hand on me, and in the words of the song "He touched me."

God is love. In Romans 5:8, God's love is described as being sacrificial. In Jeremiah 31:3, His love is described as being Everlasting. In Ephesians 2:4 it is described as being "Grrrrrreat!" Now, let me help you to understand something if I can: God is Spirit. (John 4:24) He does not embody a physical being. (John 1:18) In Psalm 110:1, the hand is figurative of God's power, in Psalm 145:16 of His provision, and in Psalm 139:10 of His protection. So, what is it about God's power, provision and protection? Let me share with you a number of indications of God having placed His hand on you.

Peace of Mind (How to stay positive in such a negative world)

7 and the peace of God, which surpasses all understanding, will guard your hearts and minds through Christ Jesus. (Philippians 4:7)

There is a peace that goes beyond anything you and I will ever understand. This is God's peace. It is this type of peace that we need while facing the trials of life. God allows things to happen the way they do on the Earth for His reasons. Because of God's holiness and love, He will not violate the free will of humanity.

If you choose to live a wild and careless lifestyle, you are free to do so. If you break the law while living carelessly, you have the penalty of what governmental authorities can do to punish you. What we must know is that when things happen that we don't understand, such as the tragedies we face in our society, God's peace can help us cope better than anything else. Not a cigarette, a drink, or any other coping mechanisms imaginable.

A Kingdom Song (How to encourage, strengthen, build up yourself and others, and smile in the process)

27 Peace I leave with you, My peace I give to you; not as the world gives do I give to you. Let not your heart be troubled, neither let it be afraid. (John 14:27)

3 You will keep him in perfect peace, whose mind is stayed on you because he trusts in you. (Isaiah 26:3)

Let's explore the words "kingdom song." First, think of what songs are and what they do. Lexicographers of past and present define a song as a musical composition or melodious utterance. Songs have certain emotions attached to them and evoke various feelings in the listeners. Usually, songs we like make us happy to hear and sing them. This scripture in the book of Isaiah is part of Israel's "kingdom song." You need to have a kingdom song. A kingdom song glorifies God and encourages the hearers. It is one that tells God how good He is, how merciful He is, how kind He is, and how faithful He is.

The word "kingdom" indicates the domain – territorial authority, sphere of influence, or place of total control – of a king. As Christians, we recognize the Lord as our King of Kings and Lord of Lords. In His kingdom, we can and should expect Him to possess total control. God has the right and authority to do whatever He wants and He chooses to bless us with His peace. When we sing kingdom songs, we allow the expression of our worries to translate into "kingdom language." It is then that our problems are placed in the hands of a worry free King who has it all under control.

Friend, when you are able to see the matchless calm God uses to take care of your concerns, you can sing in times when others are crying. You can smile, and even laugh, when you feel like screaming! You can rejoice when you should probably be breaking down. Having and singing a kingdom song will allow you to keep your mind thinking good thoughts. It will ultimately allow you to appropriate the peace that strengthens in trying times. So, the next time you're faced with a difficulty, start singing your kingdom song and watch, with your spiritual eye, as those troubles start to move in subjection to the will of Almighty God!

Now when He was asked by the Pharisees when the kingdom of God would come, He answered them and said, "The kingdom of God does not come with observation; nor will they say, 'See here!' or 'See there!' For indeed, the kingdom of God is within you." (Luke 17:20-21)

Can you recall times in your life when you had peace, and you're weren't worrying about a lot of things? That was a blessing intended for your continual enjoyment. That was God's power operating in you and on your behalf. Even now, while you're going through that "thing" you're going through (you know the thing); the power of God is holding you together. Others have literally lost their mind facing similar problems. But God allowed you to stay cool about it all. That's enough to shout about. God is even spiritually giving you an implant of the kind of peace that will allow you to remain focused in times when things can't get any worse. Have you ever felt numb after receiving such a blow? Let me share something with you: that's a shadow of God's peace also.

Picture this: A young woman is scheduled to undergo a minor surgery that involves an incision. Before the surgery takes place, the anesthesiologist will have to administer some form of medication, either by needle or gas. The purpose of this medicine is to numb the body to the obvious pain associated with the procedure.

Do you get it yet? God's peace is the anesthesia you need before going into the "surgery" of a trial in life. A problem can "cut" you like a knife also. It is His peace that <u>has</u>, <u>will</u>, and <u>is</u> allowing you to become numb so that you don't feel the obvious pain associated with the procedure. Once you get it, help others to get it also. You even have my permission to utilize this scenario to illustrate the point.

<u>Situational Victories</u> (Making things better)

57 But thanks be to God, who gives us the victory through our Lord Jesus Christ. (1 Corinthians 15:57)

4 For whatever is born of God overcomes the world. And this is the victory that has overcome the world— our faith. 5 Who is he who overcomes the world, but he who believes that Jesus is the Son of God? (1 John 5:4-5)

14 Now thanks be to God who always leads us in triumph in Christ, and through us diffuses the fragrance of His knowledge in every place. (2 Corinthians 2:14)

Have you ever gotten out of a jam and stopped to wonder, "How in the world did I get out of that one?" I know I have. At those times God had his hand on me, in spite of how badly I'd messed up. It's truly amazing to me that even when I was deeply imbedded in sin, God loved me enough to bail me out when I was in trouble. That's His nature though. (Romans 5:6-11) He made the ultimate sacrifice so that we could become overcomers. As children of God we can defeat sin and evil pleasures by trusting Christ to help us.

The word "triumph" expresses something above and beyond victory. It means to be victorious, which indicates a continuance of good things. There is only one person in the whole entire world that can do what you do better. I can introduce you to that person right now if you'll do one thing for me. Go to the nearest mirror. I'll wait... No, really. Go to the mirror... I'm serious. Come on! Go... The people sitting in the room with you might think you're a bit strange, but I won't. Are you in front of the mirror yet? Okay. Now, (insert your name), I'd like you to meet (insert your name). This is the only person in the whole entire world that can do what you do better.

Let me explain something to you. Your Deoxyribo Nucleic Acid (DNA) is uniquely different from that of anyone else's. God has designed you in a way to where the only person in the world that can do what you do better is yourself. This means that you have the potential to improve your performance, increase your knowledge, and impact lives just by being YOURSELF! Never allow yourself to be limited by the pessimistic principles that bind human progress. With Christ as the center of your focus, who knows what can be accomplished through you. That's true victory.

A Heart of Love (How to make it real)

⁵ Now hope does not disappoint, because the love of God has been poured out in our hearts by the Holy Spirit who was given to us. (Romans 5:5)

¹³ And now abide faith, hope, love, these three; but the greatest of these is love. (1 Corinthians 13:13)

As the son of a preacher, there was sort of an unspoken expectation that I would become a preacher. But, it's amazing to me that some of the kids I grew up with and used to hang out with are now saved. It's kind of hard to believe it's really them. They have completely changed. They are so pleasant! They express genuine love and concern. They always have an encouraging word.

Well, I can attest to the fact that God has placed His hand on all of us. As confirmed by 1 Corinthians chapter 13, there's a general consensus in the Kingdom of God that Love is the greatest thing on the list of all the great things to have. It's wonderful that God allows us to have this great thing called love as one of His personal actions toward us.

Success and Prosperity - The accomplishing of one's goals in life

² Beloved, I pray that you may prosper in all things and be in health, just as your soul prospers. (3 John 2)

Read Psalm 1:1-3 for background.

Writing this book was a personal goal of mine that the Lord obviously allowed to be accomplished. It was done over the process of several years of making mistakes, learning from them, and receiving encouragement from the Lord as well as mentors and friends. A word of advice: when you want to do the right thing, be careful not to take poor advice. It is such a joy to be around good people – people who will encourage you to do and be the best you can.

Whether we do it consciously or not, we set several individual tiny goals for ourselves and we accomplish them all the time. We just have to pay more attention to our many successes. Know this; God wants to get personal with you. He wants to be your personal agent, but there is a condition. You must allow God to place HIS hand on you.

God created us for "choice" worship. We are not dummies, puppets, or slaves. We have a choice. Why do you think God told Adam about the tree of the knowledge of good and evil? It was because He loves us enough to give us the power to choose to do the right thing.

You have a free will. You must make up your own mind as to whether God can take personal action in your life. You must make up your own mind as to whether He can place His hand on you.

When God's hand is upon you, people know. But you've got to get past others and deal with yourself. I submit to you today that most importantly when God's hand is upon you, YOU KNOW.

Perhaps you are struggling trying to find some peace of mind. If you don't have many situational victories, or if you need a heart of love, success and prosperity, just know that God is "the" personal agent, waiting to take personal action in your life. If you are a child of God and you don't know about the personal agency of God, perhaps you should consider allowing Him to place His hand on you. You do this by reading and studying the Word of God for yourself and by seeking His revealed knowledge.

Chapter 11

A Strategic Thinker

12 Then Jesus spoke to them again, saying, "I am the light of the world. He who follows Me shall not walk in darkness, but have the light of life."
31 Then Jesus said to those Jews who believed Him, "If you abide in My word, you are My disciples indeed. 32 And you shall know the truth, and the truth shall make you free." (John 8:12, 31-32)

We are in an age where there is a need for strategic thinkers. A strategic thinker is one who is always thinking ahead, looking ahead, and planning ahead. You need to be a part of a ministry where the leader is a strategic thinker. Strategic thinking leaders are those who:

- Help others reach their potential
- Allow people to develop their skills and talents
- Tap into people's resources and anointing that God placed within to accomplish His will
- Expect greatness from those they lead. (Even expecting them to become better than they were) In 2 Kings 2, Elijah expected

his successor to be better than he. In the book of Deuteronomy the 31st chapter, there was a greater expectation of Joshua than Moses. Even Jesus had a greater expectation of you and me, as indicated in John 14:12.

- Provides opportunities that were not provided to them. When you are a strategic thinker, you are always looking to learn more, to share more, to give more, and to do more.
- Encourages those around them to know and become part of the Vision
- Is always in the spirit (the awareness)
- Hears from God & Listens (Most important). It's important to hear from God, but it's most important to listen.

You must have a ready mind and heart, evidenced with a display of obedience to God. Just as Jesus expected His disciples to do what He said and was their ultimate example, He expects the same from us. Our obedience to God can be further exemplified in our obedience to our leaders.

The Lord says, *"If you abide in My word, you are My disciples indeed."* And He said that you're going to know the truth and the truth will make you free. Many people don't believe the truth. But the Lord says again *"If you abide in My word, you are My disciples indeed."* When Jesus said this to His disciples, He was telling them to continue in His teachings.

I have been blessed to encounter and get to know several strategic thinkers. These were men and women fervently engaged in doing what God commissioned them to do. Because of your obedience to God, you will accomplish a two-fold exchange: you will reap the benefits of a good relationship with the Lord, and you will influence others to grow and become strategic thinkers themselves.

13 Then they brought little children to Him, that He might touch them; but the disciples rebuked those who brought them. 14 But when Jesus saw it, He was greatly displeased and said to them, "Let the little children come to Me, and do not forbid them; for of such is the kingdom of God. 15 Assuredly, I say to you, whoever does not receive the kingdom of God as a little child will by no means enter it." [16] *And He took them up in His arms, laid His hands on them, and blessed them. (Mark 10:13-16)*

I now want to talk to you about some of the challenges I faced as a preacher's kid (PK). There is a bigger magnifying glass placed in front of the children of a preacher. A preacher is one who is a leader in his home, his church, and his community. Oftentimes, as the son of a preacher, I was determined to not act how people said I should act. We expect too much of our children at times.

I have three daughters. (And I don't need a shotgun! I just need your prayers) Anyway, as a parent, I'm learning that children will be children. That's all they can be. It's a fact of life. With that in mind, train them up in the way they should go. When they are of age, they won't depart from it. (Proverbs 22:6) Help them to live for today and prepare for tomorrow.

Question: How did you come to know the Lord? It was with a perfect heart and clean conscience, wasn't it? I don't think so. I'm quite certain there were some mistakes you made along the way, as we all have. With that in mind, encourage the children to make intelligent decisions. They will make mistakes. So when they do, be there to help them to learn from them and move on. The Lord wants us to become strategic thinkers. And he says *"If you abide in My word, you are My disciples indeed."*

Strategic thinking leaders are people who lead by example. They are holy men and women of God. They don't tolerate anything from the devil. They tell the truth even when it hurts. The truth sure does hurt sometimes, doesn't it? The measure of a true friend is in a person's ability to hurt your feelings <u>now</u> with the truth. This way, the devil won't be able to hurt your soul <u>later</u> with lies.

The Lord says "I have called you by my name. I have blessed you. I have anointed you. I want to separate you for a good work." You see, the Lord wants to do many great things in your life, but you have to continue in the Words of the Lord.

[49] *Behold, I send the Promise of My Father upon you; but tarry in the city of Jerusalem until you are endued with power*

from on high. (Luke 24:49)

Some of you are trying to pack up and leave the place you're in too soon. You just can't wait to leave, can you? Let me give you a little background on what I'm saying. I'm a Staff Sergeant serving in the United States Army. My job title is Human Resources Manager. As a Soldier, I've encountered people from virtually all walks of life. A constant with humans, no matter where in the world we're from, is that we're generally hard to please.

I've experienced being stationed in some great places as well as some places that were, in my opinion, not so great. The times that my stay at a place was not so enjoyable, I remember wishing I had been stationed somewhere else. I also remember God's encouragement coming to me directly or by way of a friend or mentor telling me that God had a reason for it all. Thank the Lord I listened.

Please don't get me wrong. I love the Army, and I love serving my country. My fellow comrades can attest to the same thing when I say that there have been times in my career of traveling with the military that I've wanted to stay put. There have also been times when I was ready to leave ASAP! (As soon as possible)

At any rate, I was unable to get my way every time I was ready to pack up and leave. (For whatever reasons) I will tell you that everywhere I've been in the military has been an absolute blessing. I learn more and more daily about my potential to succeed and surpass even my own expectations.

Sometimes in life, you have to do things you don't want to do. God knows our potential. He knows the plans He has for us. (Jeremiah 29:11) Growth causes change, and change can be extremely uncomfortable. When you find yourself not wanting to do something that will likely serve to help you become a better person, dig deep inside yourself and appropriate the strength you've been given by God. It is this deep inner strength, this God-breathed strength, which will allow you to be sustained and receive peace-of-mind about whatever it is you don't want to do.

In Luke 24:49 Jesus told his disciples to stay and wait for the promise of the Holy Spirit. What is He telling you to stay and wait for? If you don't know the answer to this question, don't feel bad.

It's a question many of us can't answer. If we could, we wouldn't act so hastily in our decision-making.

I can imagine how the disciples felt. After seeing all the great things that happened in Jesus' life, His ministry, His death, His resurrection, and His ascension, the disciples wanted to take on the world. But Jesus said to wait. The Lord knew that, in order to minister to the world, the disciples would need an empowerment. HE also knew that we would need the same empowerment. This is why the indwelling of and filling with the Holy Spirit has been made available to all believers who ask for it.

[16] All Scripture is given by inspiration of God, and is profitable for doctrine, for reproof, for correction, for instruction in righteousness, [17] that the man of God may be complete, thoroughly equipped for every good work. (2 Timothy 3:16-17)

The Lord wants to do a complete work in you. But if you keep trying to just punch in your clock and leave, you're going to continue to be malnourished. The only way to truly come to a place of maturity is by facing your trials head-on with integrity and a righteous resolve to overcome all odds. (In the strength of the Lord)

One of the greatest blessings to a pastor, I've learned, is when those he or she leads allow their lives to show the benefits of sound preaching and teaching. I thank God for the influence my mentors have had on my life. The benefits are much more than I can begin to express. The overflow from those benefits is what the content of this book is from. Praise the Lord!

Chapter 12

Realizing How Real the Responsibility Is

¹⁵ So when they had eaten breakfast, Jesus said to Simon Peter, "Simon, son of Jonah, do you love Me more than these?" He said to Him, "Yes, Lord; You know that I love You." He said to him, "Feed My lambs." ¹⁶ He said to him again a second time, "Simon, son of Jonah, do you love Me?" He said to Him, "Yes, Lord; You know that I love You." He said to him, "Tend My sheep." ¹⁷ He said to him the third time, "Simon, son of Jonah, do you love Me?" Peter was grieved because He said to him the third time, "Do you love Me?" And he said to Him, "Lord, You know all things; You know that I love You." Jesus said to him, "Feed My sheep." (John 21:15-17)

Jesus wanted Peter to realize how real his responsibility was. There are many things that we still have to realize. It's an ongoing, life changing process. The scripture in Acts 2:14-41 is one instance of Peter realizing his responsibility. Read this passage when you get a chance.

Let's learn how to treat one another, but let me explain some terms first. The word "real" is defined as something actual, genuine, or authentic. To realize means to bring about or make real; to fulfill, as in realizing one's potential; the bringing of an idea into actual existence. (The light begins to be turned on upstairs) Another word for this is an Epiphany- a sudden manifestation of the meaning or essence of something. Responsibility is something or someone for which one is accountable whether it is by thought, words, or action.

In the book of Acts chapter 2, verses 14 through 41, if Peter's responsibility had ended after his explanation of Pentecost, he would have left the Earth then. But it wasn't over yet. Had it ended after he healed the lame man in the 33rd chapter of Acts, he would have left the Earth then. But it wasn't over yet. Had Peter's responsibility ended after he was placed in jail, or after he was told by the Sanhedrin Counsel not to preach, or after he raised Dorcas at Joppa, or after he preached to the Gentiles and they became converted, and the list goes on, he would have left the Earth then. But it wasn't over yet.

My friend, if your responsibility had ended when you got saved, you would have left the Earth then. But it's not over yet. If your responsibility had ended when you received the fullness of the Holy Spirit, you would have left the Earth then. But it's not over yet. Brother, sister, if your responsibility ended when you witnessed to someone the other day THEN WHY ARE YOU STILL HERE? It's not over yet.

We should never stop realizing our responsibilities on this Earth. It's quite refreshing to know that we have new ideas, new challenges, fresh anointing and fresh revelations to look forward to. But we've got to REALIZE HOW REAL THE RESPONSIBILITY IS.

There are three steps to realizing how real the responsibility is:

• Seek the Lord.

What does it really mean to seek the Lord? Seeking God means that you're trying to reach Him, have an intimate experience with Him, to go toward Him, to make a request of Him. The only way to be able to reach God is to have your heart fixed and your mind made up that you will reach Him. We need to find out what God wants. If we listen carefully, He will tell us.

1 Chronicles 28:9 says *"As for you, my son Solomon, know the God of your father, and serve Him with a loyal heart and with a willing mind; for the Lord searches all hearts and understands all the intent of the thoughts. If you seek Him, He will be found by you; but if you forsake Him, He will cast you off forever."* The "know" in this scripture most likely means, "to have an intimate relationship with." We know that God chose Solomon to build His temple, and He has chosen you for something particular as well. Be strong and faithful to the work He chose for you.

As you seek God, He will open up the eyes of your heart and cause you to see a bigger picture. Pray this prayer with me: "Open my heart, Lord, and allow me to see what you are doing in me." You see, God knows the sincerity of your heart and He received that prayer based on your relationship with Him. (James 5:16)

- Obey the Lord.

This is a big one. Obeying suggests an accepting of authority. We've got to learn to comply with God's instructions. The primary way He speaks to us is through the Word of God (the Bible). You first have to believe in the inerrancy of the scriptures, (meaning that they are God-breathed, and thus free from error) and that all scripture is given by inspiration of God, is profitable for reproof, correction, doctrine, instruction in righteousness. (1 Tim. 3:16) Then you have to act upon those beliefs by doing what God tells you to do.

Ecclesiastes 12:13 says *"Let us hear the conclusion of the whole matter: Fear God, and keep his commandments: for this is the whole duty of man."* *(KJV)* You know, too many times we seek deep philosophical interpretations of what God is calling the BOTTOM LINE. "Fear me and keep my commandments"

- Trust the Lord.

This trust means having total confidence in the integrity, ability, and character of God. This trust means relying on the Omniscience of God- He knows it all, the Omnipresence of God- He is everywhere, the Omnipotence of God- He is all powerful, and His eternal Sovereignty- He, whose beginning was from eternity and whose ending goes to eternity, will always do what He sees is best. It needs to hit us like a ton of bricks that God has it all under control. We can only imagine with our finite minds the infinite wisdom of God.

When you trust in God, He works on your behalf. 1 Corinthians 2:9 says *"But as it is written: Eye has not seen, nor ear heard, Nor have entered into the heart of man The things which God has prepared for those who love Him."* Verse 10 says, *"But God has revealed them to us by his Spirit. For the Spirit searches all things, yes, the deep things of God."* If we could only catch the revelation of what God has prepared, that within itself would be a realization of the reality of our responsibility.

12 For the eyes of the LORD are on the righteous, and His ears are open to their prayers; but the face of the LORD is against those who do evil." (1 Peter 3:12)
9 For the eyes of the Lord run to and fro throughout the whole earth, to show Himself strong on behalf of those whose heart is loyal to Him. (2 Chronicles 16:9a)
8 "For my thoughts are not your thoughts, nor are your ways My ways, says the LORD. 9 for as the heavens are higher than the earth, so are My ways higher than your ways, and My thoughts than your thoughts." (Isaiah 55:8-9)

The question is do you trust Him? The Lord must be involved in every aspect of our realizing the reality of the responsibility. Philippians 2:13 says *"for it is God who works in you both to will and to do for His good pleasure."* Hebrews 13:20-21 reads *"Now may the God of peace who brought up our Lord Jesus from the dead, that great Shepherd of the sheep, through the blood of the everlasting covenant, make you complete in every good work to do His will, working in you what is well pleasing in His sight, through Jesus Christ, to whom be glory forever and ever. Amen."* Ephesians 1:5 says *"having predestined us to adoption as sons by Jesus Christ to Himself, according to the good pleasure of His will,"* which means our purpose was "mapped out" for us long before we even came into existence. That's awesome! Learn your responsibility.

A lot of times, people don't want to know their responsibility; because that means that they will have some work to do. In the body of Christ today, there are selfish individuals who only want blessings for themselves & no one else. We need to know what the Lord is calling us to do. There are two (2) keys that will allow you to walk into the realization of your responsibility.

Key # 1 – Awaken to righteousness.

34 Awake to righteousness, and do not sin; for some do not have the knowledge of God. I speak this to your shame. (1 Corinthians 15:34)

Pastor George Robinson, a friend and mentor of mine, once said, "The world is going to Hell but the church is sleeping." I admit that I really didn't grasp what he said in it's totality until I began to minister in various places and examined the state of the world around me. Romans 13:11-12 says *"And do this, knowing the time, that now it is high time to awake out of sleep; for now our salvation is nearer than when we first believed. The night is far spent, the day is at hand. Therefore let us cast off the works of darkness, and let us put on the armor of light."*
We, the body of Christ, have to wake up to what's going on. We have to take our rightful place on the Earth and begin to share the gospel of Jesus Christ so that deliverance can come to the masses. The Lord is preparing us to do this, first because He is God and He will use whomever He wants and secondly because we asked Him to. Not only in our private prayers, but we also ask Him in public worship when we sing songs like "Lord Prepare Me To Be a Sanctuary" or "You Can Use Me." There are a host of others, but these were two that came to mind as I was thinking about it. They also happen to be two of my favorites.

Key # 2 – Walk as children of light.

⁸ For you were once darkness, but now you are light in the Lord. Walk as children of light. (Ephesians 5:8)

Sadly, many Christians are struggling internally with their life as a believer in general, namely with their beliefs and walk. My friend, it doesn't have to be this way with you. If you take heed to some wise counsel, your struggle can be over. For so long, we've been surrounded by negativity. For so long, we've been pounded, poked and prodded by pessimistic principles. For so long, we have been victims instead of victors. The Bible also says here, *"And have no fellowship with the unfruitful works of darkness, but rather expose them." (Ephesians 5:11)*

Once you start exposing those unfruitful works, bringing them out into the open, you can deal with them. I challenge you to start using some scriptures of confession in your everyday life. You will start to see things change almost immediately. But don't stop there. The enemy will allow you to feel good for a little while, and then he will approach you again by the same route or another angle. That's why you have to pray, fast, read your Word, and be prepared for his attacks. Feed your faith. Starve your doubt.

Please don't misunderstand what I'm about to say: We must learn to avoid certain people while going about our daily business. 1 Corinthians 15:33 says *"Do not be deceived: evil company corrupts good habits."* What that means, child of God, is that if you are professing to have a relationship with the Lord Jesus and you are still hanging out with your old friends who still like to curse, drink, and party, sooner or later one of the two (your name)'s will come forth, the old (your name) or the new (your name). I'm not telling you to forsake your friends totally. However, if they have more influence on you than you have on them and they're not trying to do right or be right then you don't need to have fellowship with them because the relationship that was once rewarding by worldly principles is not fruitful anymore.

The questions that remain on the table are; will you seek Him, obey Him, and trust Him? You know, none of this means anything to you if you don't know the Lord. Zephaniah 2:3 says, *"Seek the LORD, all you meek of the earth, who have upheld his justice. Seek righteousness, seek humility. It may be that you will be hidden in the day of the LORD'S anger."* You must have a relationship with the Lord.

There will be a judgment. Ecclesiastes 12:14 gives a warning: *"For God will bring every work into judgment, including every secret thing, whether good or evil."* Not only do we have to realize how real the responsibility is, but we also must realize that Heaven is real and Hell is real. God does not want you to end up in Hell, but because of His righteousness and His justice, He will allow you to go if that is the decision you make. So, it boils down to a decision. Read Romans 10:8-10 and choose life eternal.

Endnote

[1] *Robinson*: From the Sermon "Sleeping in Dangerous Times," 1999.

Chapter 13

Harmony in This Present World

Be of the same mind toward one another. Do not set your mind on high things, but associate with the humble. Do not be wise in your own opinion. Repay no one evil for evil. Have regard for good things in the sight of all men. If it is possible, as much as depends on you, live peaceably with all men. (Romans 12:16-18)

God will perform the things He's been longing to perform in our lives and on our behalf once we become the Church that we have for so long said we are. John 13:34-35 proclaims *"A new commandment I give you, that you love one another; as I have loved you, that you also love one another. By this shall all men know that you are My disciples, if you have love for one another."*

Why does Jesus want the world to know we are His disciples? I believe it is partly because He knows that once people see something good, they will want to be a part of it. 2 Peter 3:9 confirms that The Lord wants all to have an opportunity to come to repentance.

God is giving sinners more time to repent because of His grace and mercy toward us. His grace is what gives us more than we deserve. We deserved death because of our sins, but God gave us a chance at life eternal instead. God's mercy was shown to us when The Lord decided not to carry out the punishment we truly deserved.

⁵ Now may the God of patience and comfort grant you to be like-minded toward one another, according to Christ Jesus, ⁶ that you may with one mind and one mouth glorify the God and Father of our Lord Jesus Christ. ⁷ Therefore receive one another, just as Christ also received us, to the glory of God. (Romans 15:5-7)

Can there be harmony in this present world? The answer is YES.

The condition of humankind and society in general presents a series of problems. We could spend all day talking about all of them or we can narrow it down to man's separation from God because of sin. But there is an answer. There is a remedy. Let's look at some more principles.

Our friends in the profession of lexicography, Webster in particular, define harmony as agreement, a combination of musical notes to make chords and a melodious sound. God wants us to make a melodious sound. From this one word HARMONY, which is a derivative of the Greek word "harmonia," you get the word harmonious, and harmonica – defined as various musical instruments. Finally, to harmonize means to bring into harmony or to be in harmony.

When you look at this, you see a music lesson in the making. Let's bring it in and gain a spiritual perspective though. We are a variety of instruments made by God for the purpose of Worship. Not only is He allowing worship to happen individually, He's allowing it to happen corporately (in the body of Christ). So that's where the harmonizing comes in.

God wants us to bring it all together (gifts, talents, anointing) in agreement. Regardless of the fact that one sings, another greets people, another exhorts, another passes out tracts, and another shares from the scriptures. Let us bring it all together for the glory of God and take it to the world. I'm talking about HARMONY IN THIS PRESENT WORLD!

We can't have harmony in this world, however, if we don't have harmony in the body of Christ. So we must focus on achieving harmony in the body in addition to working on achieving harmony in this world. But WAIT A MINUTE! How can this be done? Well, if there is harmony in your body physically, there can be a sense of harmony in your world physically.

If we can achieve and experience harmony in the body of Christ, it can spread to our work places, homes, businesses, factories, restaurants, shopping malls, grocery stores and gift shops. What a pleasant thought. But do you know what? Some people are just too scriptural for their own good. Some are afraid to do the necessary things to bring about harmony in the world because they know that these events would lead to what has been prophesied to happen in relation to the antichrist and the tribulation period and the "Left Behind" scenario.

Now, before I go further, I have to explain that there are several varying views of the end of the world. I encourage you to study the Bible for yourself to find out what the Lord says about the subject. I choose to believe it's going to happen whether we get on board or not. No man knows the day or hour (Matt.25:13) but when He comes you're either ready or you're not. Don't you want to be ready? HARMONY!

At this point, I must deal with something. The tribulation period - all the events and chaos described that many Christians, sad to say, fear - takes place after the Lord's appearing in the sky, after the rapture of the Church. We don't have to go through that stuff. Just BE READY, and STAY READY! Check 1 Thessalonians 4:15-18; 5:1-11; and 1 Corinthians 15:51-53 for more encouragement.

The kind of harmony I'm referring to can take place, but some things have to happen.

• Make sure you are straight.

[11] And this is the testimony: that God has given us eternal life, and this life is in His Son. [12] He who has the Son has life; he who

does not have the Son of God does not have life. (1 John 5:11-12)

Assurance is the security of knowing that your name is written in heaven. (Romans 8:33-39; 2 Timothy 1:12; Romans 10:9-10)

- Become an intercessor.

Intercession is prayer offered in behalf of others. Read James 5:16. Prayer changes things indirectly. People have the power to change things in this world, to make a difference, to shine light in a dark corner, so we need to pray for the people because prayer changes people and people change things. Healing can come about when we pray for one another. Turn to the Lord's Prayer and look at His example of intercession. In John 17:1-26, Christ prayed for all of us, so we should pray for others as well.

- Learn how to forgive. Mt. 6:14-15; Luke 17:3; Matt. 18:22 We have to have the attitude of Christ toward one another. Christ gives an analogy to one of His disciples as to how many times to forgive someone. He told Peter to forgive until seventy times seven. I believe the Lord was saying to forgive without limits, but some of you are just on your 13th or 14th time forgiving someone. After you learn to forgive, and you've done it enough, it will become easier and easier. And I guarantee by the Holy Ghost that you'll stop counting.

- Preach and Teach Without Hypocrisy.

Acts 10:11 is a record of when Peter saw the great sheet, God tells him to preach to the gentiles. Verse 44 states *"While Peter was still speaking these words, the Holy Spirit fell upon all those who heard the word."* Notice it didn't say all them which were black, white, yellow, green, orange, or purple, living in mansions, living in the projects or living on the streets. The Word says all those who "heard."

We as believers have the ability and the authority, as given to us by Christ Himself, to preach and teach to the world. (Matthew

28:19-20; Mark 16:15; Luke 24:47) And when we sit in our churches with all of this Word on the inside of us and won't share it with anyone outside the church walls, we are walking in hypocrisy.

- Trust God. (Psalm 33:21; Psalm 119:42) Trusting in God gives us a reason to rejoice and makes way for us to receive the answers that we need. The question is do you trust Him?

This harmony can happen, but we have to want to do what is necessary to bring it to pass in our lives.

Chapter 14

Make Up the Hedge

³⁰ So I sought for a man among them who would make a wall, and stand in the gap before Me on behalf of the land, that I should not destroy it; but I found no one. (Ezekiel 22:30)

Area of emphasis: Ezekiel 22:23-31

Ezekiel, who was a priest and a prophet, ministered during the darkest days of Judah's history: the 70-year period of Babylonian captivity. This passage of scripture parallels the state of the world today. The Lord sent the people a message of judgment, but hopefully we can learn from it and cause it to become a message of deliverance for us.

Point: It's up to the Church to intercede for the world, but the church has to be right.

Intercessor – One who pleads on behalf of others.

In addition to our praying, there are some works that should be done as well. What some people in the body of Christ have failed to realize is that there are some responsibilities to this life that we live. You can't just expect to be receiving all of these good nuggets, all of this good teaching, experience this anointing that God has given you, and not have to give of yourself in some shape form or fashion.

The more you have been endowed with wisdom; you should be that much more willing to offer advice. The more you have been endowed with knowledge, the more you should be willing to teach. The more God has blessed you with; the more you should be willing to share. The more you have learned about money, the more you should be willing to give. The more you hear about tension and hostility, the more you should be ready to offer peace. The more you see a mess, the more you should be willing to help clean it up. But who's willing to rebuild the wall of righteousness and MAKE UP THE HEDGE?

You see, people talk, and when they talk, they normally say a lot of things. Some things they say are nice. Some things they say are not nice. Some things they say are funny. Some things they say are not so funny. But you know what, the things people say don't mean much of anything unless they inspire or are proven by action. It doesn't matter how good of a Basketball player I tell you I am unless you are able to see me play well. That's probably not going to happen any time soon anyway because I had to put my knees into retirement from the up-and-back rigors of "B-ball."

My point is this: The world needs more doers and fewer talkers. Look at the condition of the world. There was a report once that HIV infected needles that were planted in the handles of gasoline pumps were injuring people. It brings into reality the fact that Satan desires to destroy what goodness this world has.

There are a lot of hurting people in this world. There are some oppressed people in this world. God is looking for some "for-real" people who love Him and are willing to show His love throughout the world. And no matter what part of the world you are currently residing in, you are still responsible for offering Christ. I ask again, who's going to MAKE UP THE HEDGE?

Why else do you think God has purposed for many of you believers who are reading this to join the military? I believe it was so that you could become "Always Ready," "Accelerate Your Life," "Aim High," and be "An Army of One," because you are "The Few and the Proud" to tell the world about JESUS!

But don't shout yet, because in spite of all these great opportunities, a great number of people in the body of Christ are sleeping. As a whole, a lot of us aren't fulfilling the basic responsibility of the Christian world. (Witnessing) There are times when it is tough to read. There are times when it is tough to study. There are even times when many of us feel that we're simply chasing the time.

Let me encourage you my friend. It doesn't take much reading and studying. As a matter of fact, it doesn't take any of that to walk up to someone and say "God Loves You." It doesn't take reading and studying to give a kind word to those you come into contact with. This thing is much more than what you can show someone in the Word of God. People need genuine love and concern along with a lesson from the scriptures. It's time for the Body of Christ to get back to the things that really matter.

You might not have the time to sit down and give a person a whole dissertation of a study that you have been conducting. It's getting to the point to where we are going to have to take off our jackets, roll up our sleeves, get to the point, and JUST DO IT. Don't misunderstand me. Studying the Word of God is what makes us stronger, smarter, and wiser. God is speaking to us more through His Word than He is audibly. What He is saying to us is *"GO SHOW THE WORLD MY LOVE."* Read 2 Peter 1:5-11 for more encouragement.

Please don't think for one minute that I am telling you not to read or study, because that's not the case. God wants us to know and understand what He is saying to us. In 2 Timothy 2:15, the Bible says *"Be diligent to present yourself approved to God, a worker who does not need to be ashamed, rightly dividing the word of truth."* Many who have read this scripture in the King James Version of the Bible have equated the word "study" to its literal meaning. This has been an accepted interpretation throughout the study halls of many Bible studies I've attended.

In my life as a believer, I have found that many people don't take the time to study the scriptures further when they seem to be cut-and-dry on a subject. That's not how I am, because I'm a serious believer who wants to know what I believe.

I did an exegetical study of 2 Timothy 2:15 and found the more accurate meaning of "try very hard" or "be diligent." Now I will not engage in an argument about what the word "study" actually means, because I already know. It's a small issue. God is actually telling us both of these things in the verse anyway.

Just for your common knowledge, the word "study" in this scripture has a cross reference to the word "labour" in Hebrews 4:11; and the words "give diligence" in 2 Peter 1:10, 3:14; and the word "endeavour" in 2 Pet 1:15. (KJV) However, the "study" that many people equate this verse with is here also. Although it's not indicated by the first word "study," it is indicated by the latter part of the verse where it talks about "rightly dividing the word of truth." (KJV)

So in our dividing of the truth, we should gain an understanding of our obligations. Before we go further, we need to properly identify some of these obligations so there won't be any confusion as to what the Lord is saying. You see there is supposed to be oneness in the church. There is a way that Christians are to behave. Our lives should be considerably different from the world.

In Ephesians 4:25-31, God reaffirms that we are all a part of one another. This being the case, we should treat one another right. These are familiar scriptures that need to be rehearsed so we'll know what to say and how to say it when we're talking to people that don't have the working knowledge we have. But don't sell people short or belittle them. There are some who live on the street that will amaze you with their wealth of knowledge. Be prepared to show love, compassion, and respect anyway. You could learn a thing or two in the process.

Satan is looking for a place to stick in his two cents. But I don't want to hear a word he has to say. I want to be <u>found</u> in <u>pursuit</u> of God. (I meant to say it that way) I want to do God's will. Don't you? I want what I say to be pleasing to the Lord and to minister to those who hear. You no doubt want the same things. So, speaking in a way that country folk like me will understand, "you can't just be 'cussing' people out." Instead, use kind words that will help and bless people.

The way some people who call themselves Christians live causes the Holy Spirit sorrow. Before I point outward, I'll tell you that I had to really repent because of my bad temper. I'm just being honest about it. When you're angry and you react before thinking, it can cause negative repercussions. I thank God that I was able to pinpoint a personal struggle I was having and get the deliverance I needed from the Word of God and the encouragement of friends.

Now let's make all of this apply. Can you recall a time or two when you got angry and gave the man at the checkout counter a piece of your mind, or the lady in the clothing store or retail store when you had to return something that wasn't as good as they said it was? I used to be that way and I'm speaking in faith that this type of behavior will not be a part of my life. I'm going to be kind, tenderhearted, and forgiving, just as God forgave me.

So we're going to take some practical principles from Ephesians 4:32 and talk about them:

1. KIND

34 Then the King will say to those on His right hand, 'Come, you blessed of My Father, inherit the kingdom prepared for you from the foundation of the world: 35 for I was hungry and you gave Me food; I was thirsty and you gave Me drink; I was a stranger and you took Me in; 36 I was naked and you clothed Me; I was sick and you visited Me; I was in prison and you came to Me.' (Matthew 25:34-36)

Jesus is the best example of Kindness. Jesus referred to a future scene of judgment as He emphasized the importance of being kind to others. You never know who you are treating good or bad, so you just have to treat everybody right if you desire a reward from the Lord later. Matthew 10:42 assures us that we will be repaid for all we do for Him. (*And whosoever shall give to drink unto one of these little ones a cup of cold water only in the name of a disciple, verily I say unto you, he shall in no wise lose his reward.*)

No matter how loudly we profess our spirituality, if it is not confirmed with kindness, it is subject to be called into question. 1 John 3:17 asks *"But whoever has this world's goods, and sees his brother in need, and shuts up his heart from him, how does the love of God abide in him?"* The apostle John was teaching on love in deed and truth. Our love needs to be practical. Love is more than words. It is actions.

2. TENDERHEARTED (compassionate) "Good hearted"

Brethren, if a man is overtaken in any trespass, you who are spiritual, restore such a one in the spirit of gentleness, considering yourself lest you also be tempted. Bear one another's burdens, and so fulfill the law of Christ. For if anyone thinks himself to be something, when he is nothing, he deceives himself. (Galatians 6:1-3)

We must do our part. When you hurt, I hurt. And when I hurt, you should hurt. That's a part of sharing one another's burdens. It's easier to understand things that you've been through. Those of you who have not been very compassionate in the past and don't plan on being compassionate any time soon, just keep on living. Your life experiences play a big role in your level of tenderheartedness toward other people.

3. FORGIVING

Luke 7:36-50 is an account of when Jesus forgave a prostitute of all her many sins at the house of a Pharisee named Simon, and taught a lesson on forgiveness. Needless to say, His adversaries didn't like this but Jesus was on a mission. That's the way we have to be. This is the toughest of the three to do for many people, but it is an obligation. There's no getting around it. You must forgive. In fact, the Lord promises in Matthew 6:14-15 that He will forgive those who forgive, and not forgive those who don't. Matthew 18:33-35 also illustrates this point.

As in Ezekiel 22, there are crazy things going on today. God's principles have been violated. The integrity of the people of God is in question because of the poor examples of love and kindness. The things of God have lost their importance to many who call themselves people of God. Be careful not to treat the things of God like any other daily task. Those who should be teaching right from wrong are not doing this. The weak are taken advantage of instead of being taken care of. So let's deal with the heart of the matter.

Why have there been instances today that God has said: "but I found none?" I believe there is a captivity scenario going on in the body today. God is calling us to make up the hedge and lead this society back to the fear and reverence for Him. There has to be a rebuilding of the walls of righteousness. MAKE UP THE HEDGE.

There are some who are in prison right now and these people are sitting in the pews, and even the pulpits of America's churches. You see, this is not a physical prison with bars or walls. This is a prison of the mind. And even though these people are free to move about, they end up staying confined to a limited amount of space spiritually.

Some of you reading this have been so used to not being good enough, not being smart enough, not having enough money, and not being successful enough, but enough is enough! The only prosperous people who come out of prison are those that do just that. They come out of prison. Come out from those prison walls of your mind and stay out! You're free. If Jesus has made you free, you're free! (John 8:36)

God has other things for you to be doing, my friend, but your mind has to be renewed. You don't have to be afraid. God has it all under control. So why torment yourself? Listen, you are reading the words of a man who has gone through several things, including depression and low self esteem. It's not a fun thing to go through, but I'll tell you what: Jesus is a healer!

Make getting rid of the inadequate spirit and the spirit of depression your prayer focus. Then watch God move those things out of your way. They have got to go! In Jesus' name, Amen.

Chapter 15

Inspiration, the Sure Route to Success

[8] This Book of the Law shall not depart from your mouth, but you shall meditate in it day and night, that you may observe to do according to all that is written in it. For then you will make your way prosperous, and then you will have good success. (Joshua 1:8)

[2] Beloved, I pray that you may prosper in all things and be in health, just as your soul prospers. (3 John 2)

The route of inspiration is not necessarily the quickest route to what many people call success. However, God's kind of inspiration is the sure route because its base is a relationship with Jesus Christ and a foundation of the un-compromised, infallible and inerrant Word of God.

My experiences with the military have allowed me to do some traveling. My family and I lived in Hawaii on the island of Oahu for six years and we absolutely loved our experiences there. While in Hawaii, we came to know a few of the roads very well. Now, there are a number of roads that I could have taken to go from my home in the city of Wahiawa to the shopping center in Waikele.

I could have taken H-2 Highway to H-1 Highway, and made a right to arrive at my destination. Or, I could have taken Kunia Road to H-1, made a left, driven for a few miles, and arrived there. Or, I could have taken Kam Highway the whole way there. I found that H-2 was the quickest route, but there was often a traffic jam on the way or an accident. I found Kunia Road to be the slowest route, along with it being a fairly dangerous road to travel from time to time. This is just an observation. No offense intended to my Kama` aina friends. Using Kam Highway was approximately in between in time. There are a few stoplights in between, and it proved to be the surest and safest route for us to our destination.

In comparison, it's kind of that way with our success as people of God. Sure, there are shorter ways to get to things. But God wants us to use His inspiration as our sure route to where He wants us.

The book of Joshua begins an understanding by the people of Israel of the Godly principle of faith and obedience to God's Word. Joshua 1:8 is a record of the Lord telling Joshua *"This Book of the Law shall not depart from your mouth, but you shall meditate in it day and night, that you may observe to do according to all that is written in it. For then you will make your way prosperous, and then you will have good success."* That statement alone lets me know that there is a "good" success and a "not so good" success. We'll talk about that in a few minutes.

3 John 2 is a wish from a godly man, the apostle John, to a man by the name of Gaius. John's prayer was that he (Gaius) would have a successful and prosperous life. We're going to find out just how important God's inspiration is to our success. But first, let's think about some terms.

- Inspiration – inner impulse producing outward action. The inspiration of God is the leading, guiding, influencing, and encouraging work of the Holy Spirit in causing a person to accomplish the will of God.

- Success (in the eyes of the world) – having a lot of money and a lot of stuff. It also means having the approval of people.
- Success (in the eyes of the Kingdom) – having the approval of God on your life, while making sure your inspiration can be traced to a root in the Word of God.

You need to understand today that inspiration is not necessarily the quickest route because it deals with more than just yourself. However, it's the route that God has chosen. This route requires us to do some things along the way. It requires us to touch some lives, dry some tears, clean some scrapes, restore some relationships, and reconcile some issues. This is not a route for fakes or phonies. But it's a route for the serious believer. It doesn't take much to be a serious believer; only a made up mind. With a made up mind...Endless possibilities! In Matthew 19:26 after the Lord gave an analogy of a camel passing through the eye of a needle being easier than a rich man entering the kingdom of God. He said ...With men this is impossible; but with God all things are possible. GET INSPIRED!

The inspiration of God is quite an exhaustive subject and it will take more time, effort and prayer on your part to gain a solid understanding. Even when you feel you have a clear picture of it, you still won't cover it all. (See Isaiah 55:8-9) What I will do here and now is deal with a few specifics.

God's inspiration is evident in the lives of the people of the Bible. For example, in Judges 13:25; 14:6; 14:19 we see how the Spirit of the Lord began to inspire Samson at times and cause him to do specific things. In Jeremiah 20:9 we see that Jeremiah could not get away from the inspiration of God and mentioned that the Word was in his heart as a burning fire shut up in his bones and it caused him to move on for the Lord in spite of previous persecutions.

It takes an inner motivation to do the things that would allow one to grow. Our growth involves what we do with what we have along the road of our success journey. How we allow for growth is by making full use of the ultimate and supreme inspiration of the Word of God. There are various modes of inspiration.

God, who at various times and in various ways spoke in time past to the fathers by the prophets, [2] has in these last days spoken to us by His Son, whom He has appointed heir of all things, through whom also He made the worlds; [3] who being the brightness of His glory and the express image of His person, and upholding all things by the word of His power, when He had by Himself purged our sins, sat down at the right hand of the Majesty on high, [4] having become so much better than the angels, as He has by inheritance obtained a more excellent name than they. (Hebrews 1:1-3)

By Hebrews 1:1-3, we know that God used many different ways in many portions of time to get His Word out by the prophets. We see in this passage of scripture Christ's superiority over the prophets and how He has been appointed heir of all things. It took a sacrifice in order for Jesus to be appointed heir of all things. He could not have done it in His divinity.

That's why He came down (To be the once for all sacrifice for sins); (To be the appeaser of the justice of God); (To be the example for the world and show that it can be done). This is the same man by whom the worlds were made, the brightness of the Glory of God, the express image of His person. He alone cleansed our sins and sat down in the place of authority. Did you catch the powerful phrasing that the writer used to describe Jesus' role and authority?

So now, the inspiration of Jesus through the Word of God is what should point the way to our motivation. There's something about Jesus that makes life worth living. There is no greater love than Jesus. John 15:13 says, *"Greater love hath no one than this, than to lay down one's life for his friends."*

There are two types of motivation: extrinsic and intrinsic. We will define them both in detail, but hopefully you will make a decision to be more intrinsically motivated where it really counts. For our learning today, I will use inspiration and motivation interchangeably because what we're dealing with links these words together more than the separating factors of the definitions. It is important to understand that there are two types of inspiration: Negative and Positive.

Extrinsic motivation (Negative Inspiration) deals with what our hopes, dreams, and intentions are externally (more fleshly related and stemming from Negative Inspiration). This is an underlying factor when we do things with the expectancy of something else in return.

We apply ourselves on the job because we want to be promoted to make more money to buy more Barbie dolls for Suzie or more Turbo men for Bobby with the Kung Fu grip and the extra turbo pack or more stuff for your car stereo, or that nice headboard you've been wanting for your bed.

Extrinsic motivation deals with the tangible things of life. I send in this coupon with the $4.95 shipping and handling for this blender that I can use to make these shakes that are supposed to make me look good. EXTERNAL! Now don't get me wrong. There is a place for this type of motivation sometimes. You should want to make more money and advance in your career for the job you do. Some of you may think you get paid the perfect amount of money for what you do, but that's not how I feel. That's another book entirely though.

We're going to look at a case study of extrinsic motivation and how it can be foiled. In the book of Esther chapter 6, Haman displays his resourcefulness in providing some very key and insightful information to the king as to the protocol for honoring a man, with the arrogant and conceited hopes of him being that man. Let's find out what happened. Read verses 1-4. Haman had a chip on his shoulder because Mordecai wouldn't bow to him. Mordecai was surely thinking of the commandment of the Lord in Exodus 20:5 about not bowing down or serving any other gods. But because Haman was a heathen, he wasn't hearing that. He was overtaken by his "not so good" success. Read verses 5 through 12. There are dangers in being solely extrinsically motivated. Here's a thought: Negative inspiration will soon cause expiration.

Intrinsic motivation (Positive Inspiration) deals with what our hopes, dreams, and intentions are internally (more spiritually related and stemming from Positive Inspiration). We do things from our heart without always expecting things in return. We want to help people. We want to see people happy. We want to see the needs of people being met. Here is an example of intrinsic motivation at work. 3 John 1-8

Let's understand how and why John praised Gaius so much. Verses 3 and 4 bring out two things. 1. Gaius had the truth of God in him and 2. He walked in the truth. You see, it's not enough to know the Word. You've got to walk in it. Verses 5 through 8 talk of Gaius' faithfulness and generosity. His name was mentioned in church as being a generous giver, and it was said that his actions should serve as an example to follow, but I don't think he did it for all that.

I think it was an inner impulse of the Word of God that caused an outward action of consistent, faithful, impartial hospitality and service to those he knew as well as those he didn't know. This is truly a tribute to the godliness of this man. Study Psalm 15 to gain an understanding of the characteristics of the Godly.

The problem with many of us is there is too much familiarity with the people we're serving. When that is the case, people end up serving to be recognized or to get in good instead of doing it from the heart and God is not pleased because He doesn't get the glory out of it. It takes God's inspiration to do things from the heart. We need more people like Gaius in our lives on our route to success. We also need to follow this example of godliness and generosity. Friends and neighbors, God has shown you in His Word what you should be doing. Men and women of God have spoken into your life countless times about what you need to be doing, but the choice is yours. The ball is in your court.

Two Models have been presented in this chapter.

So, why be intrinsically motivated? Answer: Because God is pleased by it and it allows for success that does not come any other way. Intrinsic motivation pushes us closer to receiving our eternal hope. I can't say what any other person wants. I can only speak for myself and say I want to have eternal life in the presence of the Lord.

The Bible lets me know in Titus 1:2 that it has been promised by God since before the world began. We know that He cannot lie. Life is hard sometimes. It's not always easy acting on the inspiration of God. Let's be real. The flesh can get in the way of some things that God has purposed for our lives.

Suffering persecution can dissuade us from being totally obedient to the Lord. Just know what the Word says in 2 Corinthians 1:7

"And our hope for you is steadfast, because we know that as you are partakers of the sufferings, so also you will partake of the consolation." There is a prize. We do win. We do triumph. We're not just victorious. We are triumphant! (More than conquerors) You're going to need some positive inspiration on this route to success.

What you've got to do is get The Word in you. Then you need to pray and ask God to help you walk in the truth of His Word. That's the sure route to success. Allow God to inspire you to do whatever is necessary to make your life and actions pleasing to Him. He will help you! Make the right decision!

In order to understand more clearer what it means to be intrinsically motivated, you have to be able to allow God to move on the inside of you. You must be broken. You must allow God to move beyond your outer court and get into your holy of holies. There are so many spiritual walls that many of you have built against God. Not because He did something to you, but because you failed to understand His will for your life and you equate His not answering your misguided prayers as God not answering at all.

Well, my friend, it's time for a breakthrough. Get determined to allow the Lord to penetrate the stony walls of your heart so that you can be truly intrinsically motivated. It's time to make a real impact on the lives of the people around you.

Chapter 16

These Three Words:
Learn, Work, and Go

Ephesians 1:15-23
Focus on verses 18 and 19

- You can't be trained unless you learn.
- You can't be developed unless you work.
- You can't get a harvest unless you go.
- You can't begin any of it unless you are saved.

There is a call that God has placed on your life and He wants so badly for you to realize it.

Ministries that are close to military bases tend to experience a lot of transitions. Transitions should not define a ministry, however. Let me explain what I mean. Ministry must continue regardless of the challenges churches face, to include a high rate of transition. I've asked the question to a number of scholars and people whose advice I value. The question was "how does a ministry survive when it faces rapid rates of transition?" The best answer I received was from Gordon MacDonald at a conference in Honolulu some years ago. As quickly as I had asked the question and in sort of a matter-of-fact form, he answered "there's only but so long that such a ministry will have workers in place before the transition, so you simply have to plan ahead for it."

In my experiences working with various churches, I've learned that there are three things you need to do when you become a part of any ministry. You need to learn the vision, work the vision, and then you need to leave.

In a ministry where people are members for a very short time and then are transferred to another location, there's only a certain amount of time that is available to train and develop them for the harvest. According to Bishop George Henfield, the harvest is when those who have been trained and developed are able to go out and bring more in so the discipleship process can continue. The Lord wants to see so many things accomplished in your life. These three words should accompany you in any ministry to help you find your place. Learn, Work, and Go.

Learn

1 Corinthians 2:10b says *"For the Spirit searches all things, yes, the deep things of God."* It's awfully hard, however, to explain deep things to people who are hard of hearing. (Hebrews 5:11) The writer of Hebrews could have gone on to explain some things about the King and Priest Melchisedek, of whom we don't know much about in the scriptures, but the explanation was halted by the people's dullness of hearing.

By the way, we do know that Melchisedek was a foreshadowing of Jesus Christ. This dull of hearing thing is a spiritual condition that is attempting to arrest the body of Christ. We've got to have a made up mind that we will receive everything the Lord has for us.

Before we delve deeper into this, let me dispel some misunderstandings. The fact that one person has more knowledge than another doesn't make him or her better. We are all created beings, made by God primarily to accomplish worship. I am no greater than you;

you're no greater than me. God loved us the same in that He sent Jesus to die for all of us. There is, however, a difference in the call of God on our individual lives and there is a difference in the office and level of authority God allows us to stand in. With these things come a certain level of responsibility as well as honor and respect.

Every pastor, elder, minister, lay leader, and worker should be recognized and respected as such. (Reference Hebrews 13:7-17) Romans 13:7 instructs *"Render therefore to all their due: taxes to whom taxes are due, customs to whom customs, fear to whom fear, honor to whom honor."* Here's the thing though. If people are to honor and respect you (leaders) as the Bible says, you should live your lives in a manner that is worthy of that honor. Be an example. Many times the people won't learn and embrace the vision until we can come down off of our "high-horse" as leaders and resolve our issues with it. (1 Corinthians 4:6)

As I stated earlier, we also must learn who to avoid. Romans 16:17 says *"Now I beseech you, brethren, mark them which cause divisions and offences contrary to the doctrine which ye have learned; and avoid them."* (KJV) Not everyone has good intensions where you are concerned. Some people can stunt your growth as a believer with their negative attitudes and principles. So, avoid them like we avoid giving too much candy to children.

29 Take My yoke upon you and learn from Me, for I am gentle and lowly in heart, and you will find rest for your souls. (Matthew 11:29)

There are many things that people want to do. There are many hopes and dreams waiting to be fulfilled in the ministry you're part of, but you need to learn the vision first. There needs to be a settling first so that you can receive some instruction. Proverbs 4:13 says *"Take fast hold of instruction; let her not go: keep her; for she is thy life."* (KJV) The thing is a lot of people don't make instruction their life.

A number of years ago when my second daughter's arrival was fast approaching, my wife and I were attempting to put together her bassinet. There were numerous problems in the endeavor that were directly related to the universal problem at hand: we couldn't find the instructions! We had the hardest time trying to get that thing together. The side posts wouldn't snap into place. We were starting to get frustrated when, finally, we found the instructions! They were safely nestled in a pocket flap on the floor mat of the apparatus. So we quickly pulled them out and began to experience the end of our confusion and frustration. Had we tried to force the assembly without the instructions, we probably would have broken something.

The interesting thing about this is just as the manufacturer includes the instructions for assembly; God also includes instructions for our putting together. You see, the Lord gave us so many benefits. One great benefit He gave that a lot of retailers copied is the warranty. God has the greatest lifetime warranty there ever was, is, or will be. He said this to those of us saved folks before we got saved, "if you don't like your life, bring it back and I'll give you a brand new one and a free gift. And I'll also throw in an instruction manual and a personal technician in case you don't understand the manual." How many will agree to that as being a good deal? I don't know any store that will give you that type of guarantee. God is saying the same thing to you unsaved folks too. (You know who you are) Our instruction should take its root in the infallible Word of God. 2 Timothy 3:16 says *"All scripture is given by inspiration of God, and is profitable for doctrine, for reproof, for correction, for instruction in righteousness:"* (KJV)

Work

9 The things which you learned and received and heard and saw in me, these do, and the God of peace will be with you. (Philippians 4:9)

6 So we built the wall, and the entire wall was joined together up to half its height, for the people had a mind to work. 16 So it was, from that time on, that half of my servants worked at construction, while the other half held the spears, the shields, the bows, and wore armor; and the leaders were behind all the house of Judah. 17 Those who built on the wall, and those who carried burdens, loaded themselves so that with one hand they worked at construction, and with the other held a weapon. (Nehemiah 4:6, 16, and 17)

The people in the book of Nehemiah had a mind and a heart to work. What does it mean to work the vision? It means to operate in a way that lines up with the vision of whatever ministry you are a part of. Before we go further, we need to restate some facts about vision. Vision is from God. Vision is supported by God's Word. A vision from God is not designed by God to be accomplished single handedly.

One person cannot do everything. Unless you have vision for your life, you're not going to understand vision as it is given from God to a ministry, whether it is local, national or global. If you don't understand the vision, you won't be able to accomplish the vision. You can't work the vision until you have learned the vision.

Now, don't get me wrong. You can do a whole lot of things in a ministry without working the vision. If you don't properly learn the vision, then you end up working your own purposes. When your own purposes aren't fulfilled, you're frustrated.

There's a difference between the purposes of God and the purposes of man. The purposes of God are on a much greater scale. We can't even imagine what the Lord has in store. 1 Corinthians 2:9 says *"But as it is written, eye hath not seen, nor ear heard, neither have entered into the heart of man, the things which God hath prepared for them that love Him."* (KJV) (A parallel reference to Isaiah 64:4, by the way). Isaiah 55: 8 says *"For my thoughts are not your thoughts, neither are your ways my ways, saith the LORD." (KJV)* A person who truly has a heart for God will want nothing more in ministry than to fulfill the purpose of God for his or her life.

There needs to be a reawakening of God's purpose in you, a reawakening of your destiny, a refinement of your gifts, and a refinement of your calling. Find your purpose, find your destiny, and be all that God is calling for you to be.

<u>**Go**</u> (John 15:15)

You need to learn when it is right for you to go. Many people can't wait to leave the place they're in, not realizing that they may be trying to leave too soon. Your life as a child of God should impact the life of someone else. My advice to you is that you remain in a ministry as long as God allows purpose and destiny to be fulfilled in you. Isaiah 14:26-27 says *"This is the purpose that is purposed against the whole earth, and this is the hand that is stretched out over all the nations. For the LORD of hosts has purposed, and who will annul it? His hand is stretched out, and who will turn it back?"*

Only God can decide what's in store for your life. There's no reason why we shouldn't be able to leave a ministry knowing that we've done what the Lord called us to do. You know, I'm not here to judge you, beat you up, or anything. I want to encourage you to fulfill purpose and destiny while you are wherever you are, but whether or not you do, that is between you and God.

We've got to understand God's sovereignty. God will do what He wants. He has absolute right, power and authority. Romans 9:20-21 says [20] *But indeed, O man, who are you to reply against God? Will the thing formed say to him who formed it, "Why have you made me like this?"* [21] *Does not the potter have power over the clay, from the same lump to make one vessel for honor and another for dishonor?* Too many times people want to do things to change the way the Lord made them. Make up your mind to be who God called you to be.

So what if your head is long, if your lips poke out, if your ears are big, or if your teeth look funny? Just make sure your teeth are brushed, your ears are cleaned, your breath smells good, comb your hair and live for Jesus. Tell them all, "yes, I have a big head, but as much as I can I'm going to wave this big head for Jesus!" You might have crooked teeth but when the Word of God travels through those crooked teeth, pray that the message comes across straight. I'll bet the power of God will allow those words to straighten out somebody's life.

God doesn't care what you look like. Just do His will! Go where He tells you to go, when He tells you to go.

Jesus gives an invitation. He says in Matthew 11:28-30 *"Come to Me, all you who labor and are heavy laden, and I will give you rest. Take My yoke upon you and learn from Me, for I am gentle and lowly in heart, and you will find rest for your souls. For My yoke is easy and My burden is light."*

My friend, if you can find your way to the Lord and learn what He has for your life, you can accomplish the purposes of God wherever you go.

Endnotes

[1] *MacDonald*: From a direct question asked in a seminar, 2001.

[2] *Henfield*: From a private conversation.

Chapter 17

Prepare For the Harvest

Luke 5:1-11(focus vs. 4-6)

I am speaking to two people: Those of you who are saved, who have accepted the Lord into your life. (You are a part of an important move of God.) I'm also speaking to those of you who are not saved. (You can become a part of an important move of God.)

It won't be long until Jesus Christ appears in the sky and tells us to COME ON. Many people have questioned and are still questioning, "When will the Rapture of the Church take place?" 1 Corinthians 15:52 indicates to us when it's going to happen. *"in a moment, in the twinkling of an eye, at the last trumpet. For the trumpet will sound, and the dead will be raised incorruptible, and we shall be changed."* If we're just making sure we're ready and forget to try and help someone else make it, we're not being true to our commission as believers. I want to encourage you today to prepare for the harvest. Prepare to receive the hurting people! Prepare to minister to them! Prepare to meet their needs! Prepare to work! Wash your nets! Get them ready. The harvest is coming! They're coming! They're coming! I'm glad the text in 1 Corinthians 15:52 didn't say "I" shall be changed. It said "we" shall be changed. So that let's me know it's not an "I" thing but a "we" thing.

Then, there are those who make a mockery of the statement "Jesus is soon to come."

In 2 Peter 3:1-7, Peter explained that he was writing this second epistle to stir up the people's pure minds. You need to take on some wholesome thinking. There cannot be an attitude of "business as usual." We've got to prepare for the harvest. How soon we forget that God is God! The fact that God made everything we see possible should be enough for us all to understand that what HE says is going to happen. The people in Genesis didn't believe that it was going to rain. They soon found out. The prophets of Baal in 1 Kings 18 didn't believe God would answer Elijah's sacrifice by fire. They soon found out. In the book of Acts chapter 5, this man and his wife that lied about their offering didn't think anyone would know. They soon found out. Those of you that don't believe Jesus is soon to come, YOU WILL SOON FIND OUT!

We have seen the Lord do many great things in our lives and in the lives of others, but now we need just a little more encouragement to know that we can make it. God has a plan. And just because you're well versed in the Word of God, that doesn't mean you can't receive more of a clearer understanding, and a keener revelation. By the same token, don't just keep all that knowledge bottled up inside. God's purpose for allowing you to learn all of these great things was not so you could keep it inside and become spiritually obese. (I call it the "Constipated Christian Syndrome" or the "CCS") God allowed you to learn everything you learned so that you could help others.

Now, let's get back to Luke 5. Many people have looked at this scripture in a good way. There's nothing wrong with that. Most exhortations come like this: "Man, the Lord blessed them so much that the nets broke. And they had to call their buddies and say, help us and bring your nets... And God is saying that if you obey Him your nets will break because of the overflow...." Yes, that's what happened, but that's not the whole of it. You see, when the net broke, some fish were lost. But that's not how God wants it. Jesus said to Simon "Launch out into the deep, and let down your nets (plural) for a draught." Simon said ".... at your word, I will let down the net. (Singular) I know some translations say nets (plural) in both places, but please bear with me. An exegetical study will show the King James and New King James versions have the correct interpretation here. You see, at that particular time, Simon did a poor job of preparing for the harvest. You might say, "what if he only had one net?" Well if he only had one net, Jesus wouldn't have told him "let down your nets." God knows what we have. He wants you to use what you've got to get what HE wants. But let's not beat Peter up too bad. He was a new Christian at the time. He learned. Go to 2 Pet. 3:9. It says, *"The Lord is not slack concerning His promise, as some count slackness, but is longsuffering toward us, not willing that any should perish but that all should come to repentance."* Verse 10 says, *"But the day of the Lord will come as a thief in the night, in which the heavens will pass away with a great noise, and the elements will melt with fervent heat; both the earth and the works that are in it will be burned up."* So in view of this, you should take a look at verses 11-18 and heed the instructions Peter gives in how to respond.

People of God, if you're looking forward to the Lord's coming you should be found blameless. You should be walking right, studying, and sharing your faith. Prepare for the harvest. We make so many plans without even realizing that when Jesus "cracks the sky"; our plans are "out the window."

God has placed gifts and talents and anointing in you for the work of the ministry, for the edifying of the body, for the encouragement and exhortation of the brethren. (Romans 12; Ephesians 4; 1 Corinthians 12) Either way you look at it, all 3 categories of the gifts (Motivational, Ministry, and Manifestation) have something to do with encouragement and building up of the members of the body of Christ. Romans 1:11-12 Read. We should have a desire to deposit something into someone's life. Prepare for the Harvest.

6 But this I say: He who sows sparingly will also reap sparingly, and he who sows bountifully will also reap bountifully. 7 So let each one give as he purposes in his heart, not grudgingly or of necessity; for God loves a cheerful giver. (2 Corinthians 9:6-7)

35 Then Jesus went about all the cities and villages, teaching in their synagogues, preaching the gospel of the kingdom, and healing every sickness and every disease among the people. 36 But when He saw the multitudes, He was moved with compassion for them, because they were weary and scattered, like sheep having no shepherd. 37 Then He said to His disciples, "The harvest truly is plentiful, but the laborers are few. 38 Therefore pray the Lord of the harvest to send out laborers into His harvest."(Matthew 9:35-38)

1 Finally, brethren, pray for us, that the word of the Lord may run swiftly and be glorified, just as it is with you, (2 Thessalonians 3:1)

35 Then Philip opened his mouth, and beginning at this Scripture, preached Jesus to him. 36 Now as they went down the road, they came to some water. And the eunuch said, "See, here is water. What hinders me from being baptized?" 37 Then Philip said, "If you believe with all your heart, you may." And he answered and said, "I believe that Jesus Christ is the Son of God."38 So he commanded the chariot to stand still. And both Philip and the eunuch went down into the water, and he baptized him. 39 Now when they came up out of the water, the Spirit of the Lord caught Philip away, so that the eunuch saw him no more; and he went on his way rejoicing. (Acts 8:35-39)

Someone who is preparing for the harvest will do the following:

1. Give. (2 Corinthians 9:6-7) A person who wants to see God's work go forward understands that it takes money to fulfill certain requirements of ministry.
2. Recognize a need and pray for it to be met. (Matthew 9:35-38; 2 Thessalonians 3:1) It may not happen all the time, but sometimes God will have you to meet the need you prayed for. Example: When my wife and I were just friends, I prayed for her to get a good man…She got one. I'll tell the full story some other time.

3. Seize opportunities. Acts 8:35-39. Philip witnessed to an Ethiopian Treasurer (Hot-shot Banker). The man became born again and it just so happened that they passed by some water. Philip seized the opportunity and baptized him there.

Here is an opportunity for salvation....

Now, I know what some of you are saying in your minds. "I did that already. I already said what the preacher told me to say." But won't you just say it again now, and with earnest and sincere resolve to commit yourself to it? Romans 10:9 has the way. When you surrender, God will accept you and give you a fresh start.

The biggest lie that you've been told by Satan is that you have time. He doesn't mind you knowing that God is real, that Jesus is real and He saves, that Heaven is real, or that Hell is real. Satan really doesn't want you to know that you don't have time to reject the Lord's call to salvation. God is saying to you now, COME ON.

My prayer is that the LORD will richly bless you as you continue the process of learning more of His plan for your life. Until next time, be blessed.

Your friend,

Derek

CPSIA information can be obtained at www.ICGtesting.com
Printed in the USA
BVOW022009240912

301266BV00002B/45/A

9 781594 674556